IMAGES
of America

CINCINNATI POLICE HISTORY

On the cover: Taken July 14, 1910, this faithful companion rides with police chief Paul M. Milliken, most likely during one of the city's Inspection Days. Milliken was officially appointed chief on March 3, 1903. As the 21st police chief, Milliken served until October 14, 1910. In this year, the city's population was recorded as less than 363,581, and the police force was 643 officers strong. They patrolled 49 square miles. In 1911, the Police Telephone and Signal Service handled 1,081,922 service calls; proof that the city's need for a widespread police force was growing. (Courtesy of the Greater Cincinnati Police Historical Society.)

IMAGES
of America

Cincinnati Police History

Christine Mersch with the Greater Cincinnati
Police Historical Society Museum

ARCADIA
PUBLISHING

ISBN 978-0-7385-5096-1

Published by Arcadia Publishing
Charleston, South Carolina

Printed in the United States of America

Library of Congress Catalog Card Number: 2007930299

For all general information contact Arcadia Publishing at:
Telephone 843-853-2070
Fax 843-853-0044
E-mail sales@arcadiapublishing.com
For customer service and orders:
Toll-Free 1-888-313-2665

Visit us on the Internet at www.arcadiapublishing.com

This police memorial proudly stands outside on Ezzard Charles Drive, across from District 1 and behind Music Hall. It was erected in 1988. The memorial lists all the known names of fallen officers and is, just as is the intention of this book, dedicated to those who have served and given their lives to protect others.

CONTENTS

Acknowledgments

Sincere thanks go to the Greater Cincinnati Police Historical Society for all their help and for tolerating my continual questions. All photographs or documents are used with their permission. You can find out more information at their Web site, www.gcphs.com.

Also, I would like to thank my editor at Arcadia Publishing, Melissa Basilone, plus my family and friends for supporting me during this project.

INTRODUCTION

In 1890, George M. Roe wrote *Our Police*, the story of the Cincinnati Police Department (CPD). Since then, there has been no publicly produced history of the department. Now, Christine Mersch has addressed the need of an up-to-date history of this venerable police force. Her book tells the story of the department through stories and photographs of the men and women who have donned the badge to protect the citizens of Cincinnati.

Cincinnati was incorporated in 1802, and the following year an ordinance established the night watch, unpaid men who patrolled the streets. As the city grew, so did its need for better protection. Watchmen were hired—paid protectors who earned a dollar a night for their services.

Modifications to the night watch system were frequent. The system of pay, organization, and leadership changed as often as city council changed. Despite a merry-go-round of police chiefs, city marshals, and police commissioners in the mid-1800s, the police department developed and matured. Uniforms were standardized. A detective bureau was created. Military-style discipline became the norm.

The Civil War came to the doorstep of Cincinnati when Confederate Gen. John Hunt Morgan's cavalry threatened to come north from Lexington, Kentucky. Cincinnati's police were armed with muskets, assembled into militia companies, and sent south to stop Morgan. A major clash did not occur, and the policemen returned to their beats.

The first chapter of this book, Early Policing, covers the 1800s to 1919. During this time, Cincinnati police initiated formal registration of arrested persons, and created a "rogue's gallery" of offenders photographs. Call boxes with telegraphs were installed around the city, improving communication. They were replaced with telephones 13 years later. In 1881, Cincinnati became the second city in the nation to use police patrol wagons.

The CPD broke the color barrier in 1884 when it hired African American Harry Hagerman as a patrolman. However, it was not until 1899 that the CPD promoted James Allen and Frank A. B. Hall as the first African American detectives. Hall retired after a full career in 1926 and continued to serve the city as a Cincinnati city councilman.

An irony of police work is that while it occasionally requires strong men to take action, the job itself rarely affords policemen the opportunity to maintain their fitness. To continue officers' fitness levels, Cincinnati established a police gymnasium in 1886. It was proclaimed one of the best such facilities in the nation. Patrolmen were required to attend the gym regularly throughout the week, and trained in gymnastics, boxing, wrestling, and running.

Shortly after the beginning of the 20th century, the first motorized patrol wagon was introduced. Also, thanks to civil service reform, testing became the method for hiring and promoting officers. A lasting reminder of the need for civil service reform can be found in the permanent records of Cincinnati policemen employed in the late 19th century. The notation "Democrat" or "Republican" is marked in the upper right-hand corner of their records.

In chapter two, "Developments in the Department," we look at more advancements made between 1920 and 1951. During this era, formalized classroom instruction of new officers was expanded from only a few weeks to 60 days. Course work included training in first aid, criminal and civil law, physical fitness, and self defense.

Near the end of World War II, the first four women were sworn in to the CPD. They held the classification of policewoman and were assigned to the Juvenile Bureau. They carried guns in their purses and did not wear uniforms.

Chapter three, "Advances in the Force," addresses police history from 1952 to 1976. Early in this time period, the police adapted one of the Allied secret weapons in World War II—radar technology—to identify and catch speeding cars.

In 1957, *Life* published a three-part story on crime in America, trying to answer the question, "What should a city expect from police?" Col. Stanley Schrotel of the Cincinnati police was featured on the cover of the September 16th issue that year, with the line, "Chief of Cincinnati's Model Police Force." Detailing the ways in which the CPD worked to gain the public's trust, that article showed how the CPD set the standard for all the nation's police departments.

In 1965, the CPD partnered with the National Conference of Christians and Jews (now called Bridges for a Just Community) to develop a police-to-community relations program. A year later, the Community Relations Bureau was created to develop positive programs to enhance the communities' understanding of the police.

Radio technology continued to advance, and in the early 1970s, Cincinnati police officers began carrying their radios on their belts, allowing them greater freedom and improved communication. By the middle of the decade, the call boxes of the mid-19th century were all out of service.

In 1974, women were given the rank of police officer for the first time. They were trained and equipped the same as the male officers. Women wore the uniform and patrolled the beat just as men did, and were no longer relegated to only the Juvenile Bureau.

Chapter four, "Modern-Day Police Department," covers the period of 1977 to 2007. The CPD suffered a string of murdered policemen in the late 1970s, and to better protect its officers, the department issued body armor. Also, the more powerful .357 Magnum revolver replaced the .38 Special revolver in 1980. Affirmative action became a policy in CPD's hiring, and in the early 1980s, the department began to aggressively recruit females and African Americans to become police officers. The Mounted Patrol, which had been disbanded in 1942 due to manpower and supply shortages, was reinstituted.

Radio technology merged with computer technology in 1994 with the introduction of Mobile Data Terminals (MDTs) to Cincinnati's beat cars. This gave officers the ability to run computer checks on suspects without the aid of dispatchers. MDTs also allowed officers to send information to other beat cars without people being able to monitor the communication on scanners.

The CPD faced disorder in the fall of 2000 when the Trans-Atlantic Business Dialogue, an international business group, met in Cincinnati. Protestors from across the country came, many intent on violence. The CPD met the large disorderly crowds with a new technology: bean bag shotguns. This less-lethal tool stopped the rioters without causing serious, permanent injuries to the suspects. A year later, riots again erupted as people protested the police shooting of an unarmed man. One result of the ensuing investigations was the creation of the Community Partnering Center, which provides an avenue through which Cincinnati police officers work with citizens and businesses to jointly solve problems. Another result of that, and other high-profile incidents, was the introduction of the Taser, an even less lethal electronic device that delivers a low-current, high-voltage jolt to suspects.

Some 50 years after *Life* proclaimed the CPD to be a "Model Police Force" for the nation, the stated vision of the CPD is to "be recognized as the standard of excellence in policing." This book shows how the CPD has, and is, living up to that vision.

—Alan March
Greater Cincinnati Police Historical Society

One

Early Policing 1800s–1919

Valentine Heubach served on the Cincinnati Police Department (CPD) in the late 1800s. In this picture, he is wearing a Civil War uniform. After the Civil War, soldiers who became policemen continued to wear a Civil War–style uniform while on the force. Before the Civil War, many policemen simply wore badges to identify themselves as cops.

Built between 1867 and 1869, the Cincinnati Workhouse stood on Colerain Avenue. This jail was built thanks to a resolution from Cincinnati's city council on July 21, 1865, that underscored the need for a new workhouse. Land was bought in Camp Washington for $50,000, and construction started in 1867. The six acres of land also encompassed two workshops and two reception buildings, plus a brick stable and wagon house. Ira Woods, an early workhouse superintendent, also served as police chief from 1876 to 1878. The workhouse was used until the late 1980s.

The date on this flag represents a change in the police department from hiring by political appointments to hiring through an early form of civil service. On this date, everyone in the department went under review; officers either kept their old rank, were reduced in rank, or were dismissed. The stripes on the flag represent the Ohio River. On the wreath are Oak leaves (on the right) and Laurel Leaves (on the left). Buckeye leaves, a symbol for the state of Ohio, are on the top.

This Gatling gun helped stop the major riot in Cincinnati. Named the 1884 Hamilton County Court House Riot, this conflict was actually sparked by the December 24, 1883, murder trial of William Berner and Joseph Palmer. Both men murdered their employer, Kirk, but when they went to trial, the jury found Berner guilty of the lesser charge of manslaughter. Citizens rebelled, believing that evidence against Berner was tampered with to assure him a lighter sentence and rule out the death penalty. A group of Cincinnatians met at Music Hall to protest, but their anger over the trial grew and they marched on the courthouse, setting it on fire and destroying it. The riot lasted for three days, and was finally quelled by the Cincinnati police with help from the Ohio National Guard. About 50 people died in the fray, and another 200 were injured.

Installed in 1866, these locked call boxes held a telegraph system that officers used to tap messages to a central operator. In 1879s, these boxes were updated with a telephone connected to a city hall operator. Officers had to check in every hour while on patrol. Individual radios completely replaced call boxes by 1971.

Police officers stand inside the police gymnasium, located on the third floor of city hall at this time. The police gymnasium officially opened in 1886 at the Hammond Street Station with A. C. Brendamour as the first director. It moved to city hall in 1900. In 2007, many police officers work out in a weight-room inside the police academy at Gest and Evans Streets, where Spinney Field (the old Bengals training field) used to be.

These police officers from District 5 pose for a quick picture. It is believed that this picture, as well as the next two, was taken in 1886 when these photographed police officers were promoted. In this picture are, from left to right, Sgt. John H. Kiffmeyer, Sgt. Louis Schmitt, and Sgt. Edward C. Hill. All three men were promoted from patrolmen to sergeants in 1886. Kiffmeyer and Hill were both contenders for the Morgan Medal—an honor named after Robert J. Morgan, former president of the board of police commissioners. Morgan himself created the medal to credit outstanding police officers. Five different medals were given in these early police days: the Morgan, the Wing (named after Col. Charles B. Wing, another president of the board of police commissioners), the Alms, the Longworth, and the Henshaw, which was strictly for valor.

This lavish roll of honor certificate was given out from 1888 to the early 1920s for heroic acts accomplished by police officers. Each color lithograph was highly personalized; notice that this one prominently displays the officer's badge number. Also important to take note of are the dress belt and baton, handcuffs, and oil lantern. The handgun is a great depiction of the first metallic cartridge revolver used by the department. These color lithographs may have been awarded to officers during a public presentation, typically in front of the entire police department and the mayor. This roll of honor was given to William C. Boers Jr. for stopping a team of runaway horses at the corner of Central Avenue and Sixth Street. Boers joined the force around 1886 and received many commendations during his career as a police officer.

Unlike Valentine Heubach, Cincinnati police officer Joseph Thornton is wearing a post–Civil War uniform, so this picture must have been taken around 1900. The first police officers worked in their own clothes with just a badge for identification, until a general uniform code was adopted in 1856. After the Civil War, in 1886, the uniforms still varied greatly, depending on an officer's rank, although most outfits required a dark blue overcoat over plain white, collared shirts. Pins and buttons on the outside jacket showed rank, district, and other information about individual police officers. In 1928, a uniform similar to today's style was adopted, and a .38 caliber revolver was added to a policeman's must-have list. Police uniforms continued to evolve slightly over the years, and different uniforms for winter and summer use were adopted and evolved. In 1970, a new Eisenhower jacket (for use with the new radios), new gun belts, and holsters were issued along with the basic uniform.

Roscoe Lewis, a Cincinnati mounted police officer, poses with his police horse. Mounted police officers started supplementing foot patrolmen in 1886. The mounted patrol was disbanded around the 1930s, due to changing needs in the department. The horse patrol was reinstated in 1988, and continues to serve the city in 2007.

Policeman George LePoris died on November 12, 1917. On that day, detective Albert W. Wegener responded to a call about a suspicious individual trying to pawn a watch at a shop on Central Avenue and New Fifth Street. Wegener found the suspect, who instantly opened fire, killing the detective before he could reveal the suspect's name. LePoris was among the many officers called for backup, and LePoris was killed by friendly fire.

William H. Moffitt (shown on the left) was a cavalry patrolman sworn into the police department on January 30, 1888. This photograph was taken at the District 6 police station at Tennyson and Eastern Avenues. Moffitt joined the more than 400 other Cincinnati police officers working for the city at the time.

Moffitt retired on September 27, 1921, after 33 years on the force. He had three children, Ella (Moffitt) Byrne, Harry William Moffitt, and Albert Moffitt, and three grandchildren, Harold Byrne, Albert Byrne, and Ruth (Moffitt) Stump. It was Ruth who donated this information, and a selection of guns, to the Greater Cincinnati Police Historical Museum. William died of natural causes in 1932 and was survived by his wife, Anna (Trosst) Moffitt.

Probably taken in 1890, this picture shows Edwin S. Goepper, a police officer who was appointed on May 14, 1887. Goepper worked in District 2, otherwise known in those days as Hammond Street Station because of its location. Early on, districts were named for their street location. In 1914, the district moved to 314 Broadway, and operated as a police academy. The station closed in 2004.

The District 4 station was built in 1892 at 754 West Fifth Street and remained active until 1955. A patrol house—a small police station that housed police-owned horses—stood near this location. A plaque still hangs above the door, listing officers of that time: police commissioners James Boyle, Milo C. Doods, Thomas C. Minor, and Lewis Werner; Mayor John B. Mosley; and superintendent of police Phillip Deitsch (he served 1886–1903).

Fred Hess became a sergeant on April 30, 1897, and worked at District 8; this picture was taken before 1904. District 8 was built in 1895 at 2616 Vine Street. Situated at the top of a hill, the building was ideally located for police horses that patrolled the upper Clifton area—this way they did not have to walk to a downtown horse station.

The first bicycle Cincinnati police squad started in 1897. This picture of John B. Muhle (left) and Jacob Sterley was taken in June of that same year. Bicycle officers were also referred to as "mounted patrol," a term that also encompassed officers patrolling on horseback and wagon drivers. The bicycle squad was so successful that two years later they expanded to patrol outlying districts.

These two police officers—Aaron J. "Tip" Nightingale on the left, with his moustache turned down, and Henry Kuhn on the right, with his moustache turned up—are both wearing a "mourning badge," which was worn anywhere between 4 to 10 days after a notable figure's death. Nightingale was an officer from April 19, 1904, to February 1932, and Kuhn worked from January 22, 1901, to August 16, 1932.

Officer Webster Roberts was a Lockland Ohio policeman around 1900. His badge is styled after that of the CPD's badge during those years. As one of the largest towns, Cincinnati's police department was on the forefront of style and technology. Policemen as far as Florida, Iowa, and West Virginia used this style of badge up until 1976. At that time, many departments started designing their own badges.

Officers pose outside Patrol House No. 2 on 408 McAllister Street with their loyal dog sometime between 1881 and 1913. Thomas Duffy stands on the far right of the picture. Duffy entered the CPD on May 12, 1881, as a patrolman. He was promoted to lieutenant in July 1884, and became superintendent of police on November 22, 1883, a position he held until February 1, 1911. He rose through the ranks of the police department and commanded District 8, which patrolled the neighborhoods of Clifton, Mount Auburn, and Corryville. Duffy died in his home at age 61, presumably of heart failure. At that time, he was one of the oldest commanding officers. Patrol wagons, like this one in the picture, were first purchased in 1881 to assist men on their beats, carry reinforcements, transport prisoners, the wounded, and the dead, and aid fireman. Cincinnati was reportedly the second city in the United States to use patrol wagons in policing. But by 1913, patrolling via horse-drawn carriages was obsolete, and they were phased out.

It is believed that Frank A. B. Hall (shown here) was appointed to join James A. Allen, both African Americans, on the detective squad. Allen became a policeman in 1886, and was appointed as the first African American detective in 1899. Born in Kentucky, Allen worked for Robert Morgan, the head of U.S. Playing Card Company who later became a police commissioner. Morgan helped Allen apply for the police department as soon as African Americans were eligible. Henry Hagerman was the first African American police officer to work in Cincinnati. He was hired in 1884 by the Democrats, who had recently taken political control, to spite the Republicans. By 1899, the need for an African American detective arose, and the position was offered to Bill Copeland, then a deputy sheriff. He declined the position, but nominated Allen. By 1926, there were 27 African Americans working on the force in various capacities. Hall joined the force in August 1898 and was also the first African American, former police officer elected to city council.

The tale of Handsome the dog begins in the late 1890s. Patrolman "Big Jim" O'Neill (shown on the left of this picture) was making his rounds on the riverfront beat when he found Handsome shivering and hiding from the rough weather. Big Jim rescued him, and legend holds that the two became good friends and partners. Handsome served District 2, first when the station was located at Hammond Street and continued when the station moved to Broadway. Handsome worked with Big Jim for about 14 years, patrolling "rat row" along the Ohio River bank in the Cincinnati "bottoms" neighborhood. He even assisted in many arrests; detective Capt. Patrick Hayes tells the story of when he was a rookie patrolman and Handsome helped him catch a fleeing suspect. Handsome attended his final roll call around 1912 before passing away, and Big Jim was killed in the line of duty in 1915.

This early photograph was taken sometime before 1904. The third man from the right in the second row is John Thomas, an early African American police officer. He was described in the 1901 Cincinnati Police and Municipal Guide as educated, gentlemanly, and extremely competent at his job. The guide also states, "It would be hard to find a more perfect model of physical manhood." It is apparent that this picture was taken during this time because of the officer's large badges and bobby hat style of head wear. In 1904, officers were issued smaller badges, and a few years later, police officers switched from wearing bobby hats to a more contemporary flat-top hat style. The superintendent of police at this time may have been Philip P. Deitsch (who served from 1886 to 1903), or Paul M. Milliken (who took over in 1903 and changed his lead title to chief of police, a title that is still used today).

District 9 is shown here in 1908, and it was built in 1907 at 3201 Warsaw Avenue. During consolidation efforts in 1927, District 3, which was previously at 73 East McMicken Avenue, moved to District 9, and District 9 was renamed District 3. Built to match the architecture of the next-door library, this district building is still used as an active police station in 2007.

Officer Frank Korte was born December 13, 1885. He joined the police force in 1913, the same year the Motorcycle Squad was introduced. Korte married Rose and left the force on July 1, 1942, right in the middle of World War II. The force, at this time, saw a decline in the number of police officers due to the draft. In order to attract more young men, revolvers were issued to police recruits.

This photograph was taken around 1915–1918. Seated are, from left to right, lieutenants Imwalle, Ringer, and John Seebohm. Standing are, from left to right, sergeants Emmett Kirgan, Frank McNeal, and Peter J. Schroder. Ringer was first appointed to the force on June 8, 1891, and Schroder was promoted to sergeant in 1915, then lieutenant just three years later. Kirgan and Seebohm were both promoted to the rank of major in 1928.

Annie Hart was the first female officer in the United States to die in the line of duty. A matron of the local women's jail, she was beaten to death by inmate Reuben Ellis—a 28 year old jailed for burglary—on July 24, 1916, at 5:00 p.m. It is believed that she was beaten to death during Reuben's attempted escape. He was executed February 6, 1917.

Officer Oscar Deckert sits atop his horse. Appointed on April 1, 1916, Deckert also joined the police force as a substitute patrolman. After a 90-day probationary period, he was assigned to the mounted patrol at District 1. A few years later, around 1919, Deckert suffered an injury when his horse slipped and fell on top of him. He retired from the force on August 1, 1950.

George Tepe joined the force as a substitute patrolman in 1901, although this picture was taken much later. In December 1902, Tepe was nominated to become a patrolman contingent on a passing grade on the examination. He passed in January 1903 and worked as a mounted police officer in Districts 10 and 3. He officially retired on October 1, 1944.

Charles Tritschler was a Cincinnati police officer from March 24, 1908, to June 1, 1952. This picture was taken around 1918. His most notable arrest was that of Martin Hamman and Charles Schwibbe, two well-known counterfeiters in those days. Tritschler recovered $9,000 in phony $10 bills that they planned to distribute during busy Christmas shopping days.

This officer carries an early lantern used by the Cincinnati police. In those days, two lanterns were typically used: a larger lantern was carried by hand, and a second style, smaller, could be attached to the officer's gun belt. It is rumored that officers would carry the lanterns in their jackets to keep them warm when not needed. In 1888, a Cincinnati police inventory lists 160 lanterns used by officers.

From 1896 to 1957, District 5's police station stood at 1024 York Street. District 1 was stationed in this building for some time before moving in 1955 to its present-day location at 310 Lincoln Park Drive (the street was later renamed Ezzard Charles Drive). In 1957, District 5 was forced to move to 1012 Ludlow Avenue due to poor building conditions and expansion. In 2007, District 5 still stands there.

The Cincinnati police wrestling team includes, from left to right, (first row) Charles Tritschler, Harry Behr, and Mr. Pool; (second row) Bill Nimmo, Fred Polts, Joe Myler, and Chester Wright. Tritschler was on the Cincinnati wrestling team from 1905 to 1910. He also joined the Holy Name Society (a Catholic organization) and the Cincinnati Retired Police Association.

Built around 1900 at Spring Grove and Hoffner Streets, the District 10 building no longer stands. Up until 1927, the CPD had 10 stations, but after this date, they consolidated. In 1902, the numerical strength had grown to 536 officers to serve a population of approximately 330,000. An annual report written that same year lists 10 police and 10 patrol stations in Cincinnati.

District 7 was built on the corner of Concord and Morgan Streets in the early 1900s. In 1930, they moved to 813 Beecher Street, where they stayed until 1976 (this picture was taken in 1969). District 7 and District 4 (then at 7017 Vine Street after moving in the 1950s) consolidated into a new District 4 at 4150 Reading Road in 1975–1976. In 2007, this remains the newest district building.

Maj. Charles Wolsefer joined the force in 1904 and worked at District 1 for many years. Wolsefer was promoted to corporal in 1909 and was later promoted again to the position of sergeant in 1910. In this position, he worked as a mounted police officer in District 3. During his time on the force, he also worked on the traffic patrol and safety patrol. On February 12, 1938, he was promoted to police major, which at that time was the title given to all district superintendents. This picture must have been taken after his promotion to traffic superintendent, since he is wearing a safety patrol patch on his sleeve—in those days, one's first patch was placed low on the sleeve, and subsequent promotional patches, stripes, or badges were placed above it. Wolsefer finally retired from the force on January 16, 1942.

Taken during Inspection Day on October 14, 1905, this picture shows the grand police force at attention in downtown Cincinnati. Around the beginning of the 20th century, the Cincinnati police force employed 528 men and made 13,291 arrests. Of those, 405 were felony charges, 9,554 were misdemeanors, 2,592 were made for the general safekeeping of the town, and 58 were charged with lunacy.

Policemen stand in the Redlands Field (which became Crosley Field, home of the Cincinnati Reds until 1970) before an annual inspection. A huge, city-wide event, each inspection was lead by the head of police (either the chief or superintendent, depending on the year) and the police inspector. Often the major political players of the day would be on hand to watch the police perform their maneuvers, including mayors, governors, and other dignitaries.

At the beginning of an annual inspection around 1905, policemen stand in the Redlands Field. For any police department, their annual parade, inspection, and review day, commonly referred to as Inspection Day, was an extremely important event. A newspaper article from October 10, 1911, states that that year's Inspection Day would take place in Cincinnati on Saturday October 14. The large police group required to perform in the parade included Companies A–K, the color guard, troop, Auto Patrol, motorcycles, and 10 patrol wagons. They assembled at city hall at 9:45 a.m. on Saturday, and their uniform code for the parade was posted in the newspaper so that all members looked their best. Company M was assigned to work their regular shifts during the parade, so even though this was an annual event, not all officers participated. Other pictures found in the police museum show that other Inspection Days were held in the Cincinnati Redlegs baseball stadium and near present-day Eden Park.

Probably taken between 1901 and 1905, mounted police officers practice their maneuvers in Eden Park near the Mount Adams area. In 1904, Officer William H. McDermott was nominated as the first mounted officer to direct traffic. McDermott was promoted to sergeant in 1930 and retired from the CPD in 1942. He died in 1964.

On October 16, 1907, a streetcar jumped the tracks at Elberon and Mount Hope Roads and crashed into this house. Harry H. Bausch was killed, and at least 18 others were injured. It was noted that about 50 people were on the car as it tumbled off the tracks, although many of the passengers were able to jump to safety.

The Police Sub Station No. 7 was just a small outpost in November 1908, stationed at Vine Street. Around 1902, there were nine other substations: ranging from No. 1 at 316 George Street, No. 4 at 748 West Fourth Street, No. 6 at Columbia and Delta Avenues, and No. 8 at McMillan and Ravine Streets.

Anton Bachman was killed in the line of duty in 1908. Bachman's great-grandson Robert Ruehlman was a Cincinnati common pleas judge best known for his decision in the Marvin Warner case. Warner owned the Home State Savings Bank, which collapsed in 1985 as a result of Warner's investments in a fraudulent securities firm. Judge Ruehlman sentenced Warner to the Madison Correctional Center in Lebanon, Ohio, in April 1991.

A police drill on June 9, 1908, occurred on Florence and Reading Roads. It is interesting to note the large signs on the side of the road, advertising for local businesses. A few years after this inspection, the board of public safety was abolished and a director of public safety was appointed to assume charge of police and fire departments.

Police officers fall in line at a 1908 police inspection. In this photograph of the police force at that time, Chief Paul M. Milliken stands on the far left, and inspector John Carroll stands in the center right. Milliken served until 1910, when he was replaced by Col. William H. Jackson as police chief. Appointed by the city's council, Jackson was removed two years later due to alleged incompetence.

William Howard Taft, a Cincinnati native, smiles after hearing he was nominated for president. Deemed Notification Day, this picture was taken on July 28, 1908, outside of Taft's home. As a lawyer, Taft worked hand in hand with the police department. This picture was taken outside Taft's house, which, in 2007, is the Taft museum in Cincinnati.

The Tyler Davidson Fountain, which was dedicated in 1871 to the people of Cincinnati, can barely be seen in this photograph taken on Inspection Day, October 3, 1908. Inspection Days died out after policemen went on strike in 1918. They protested low wages and having to buy a dress uniform with their own money that they only used once a year for Inspection Day. Five officers were suspended as a result.

A Republican who was elected mayor of Cincinnati in 1908, Leopold Markbreit died just a year later on July 27, 1909, at 11:00 p.m. This picture was taken on July 30, 1909, when the entire city filed out to watch his funeral procession, complete with police escort, as it passed down Eighth Street. Born in Austria in 1842, Markbreit served for the Union during the Civil War before becoming mayor.

These police officers are shown inside District 8 around 1910. Fred Hess stands on the far right. Notice the mix of hats: the traditional bobby hat style was reserved for men on foot patrol, and the more modern, flat-top style of hat was often assigned to patrol wagon drivers.

George Egloff stands in the center of this picture, which was taken after 1904 at a get-together at Egloff's home. While most of these officers are probably off-duty, in those days, it was common to wear one's uniform even when one was not working. During his time on the force, Egloff worked at Districts 2, 3, and 9, and on the motor patrol.

The Police Colts baseball team may have been named for the Colt handgun issued to all police officers during this time. Egloff sits on the ground on the right in the first row of this picture. Egloff joined the force on May 1, 1915. At this time, he weighed just 150 pounds and was five feet, five inches tall. He was later appointed an officer by director of public safety John R. Holmes.

These detectives took a group shot outside of Cincinnati's city hall sometime between 1915 and 1920. The bureau consists of the officers pictured here: Sherwood (1), Frame (2), Weiss (3), Knockenhauer (4), Heisterman (5), Beckrogge (6), Beckman (7), Gier (8), Schaefer (9), Wagner (10), Ottoway (11), H. Studer (12), Horsseter (13), Reikert (14), Schutle (15), Hall (16), Bell (17), O'Brien (18), inspector of detectives Cal Crim (19), Pflug (20), Hayes (21), Heufflein (22), and Baldwin (23). Crim joined the force in 1886 and served for eight years before joining the detective bureau. He was said to have a natural inclination for this sort of work and, hence, became nationally known for his detective work. He was promoted to sergeant of detectives in 1900, and 13 years later, he became the group's inspector. He worked closely with Chief William Copelan to decrease the amount of crime in Cincinnati. Through his exceptional work, he led the detective bureau so well that they consistently won recognition all over the country.

Two

DEVELOPMENTS IN THE DEPARTMENT 1920–1951

Taken in 1920 at Sixty-ninth and VanKirk Streets in Carthage, Martin W. Steiner poses for a picture. During this year, Steiner was a member of the 696-strong city police department that served a population of 401,247. During his career, Steiner worked for Maj. Michael Kane, the director of School of Instruction—a precursor to the Cincinnati Police Academy.

Cincinnati city manager C. O. Sherrill announced on June 18, 1926, that police officers would start carrying cameras, such as this one hidden inside an officer's nightstick. Obviously these cameras would help gather solid evidence against a suspect, but Sherrill also had another plan; he wanted to develop a "city reproduction plant" to collect high-quality photographs of area parks and municipal buildings.

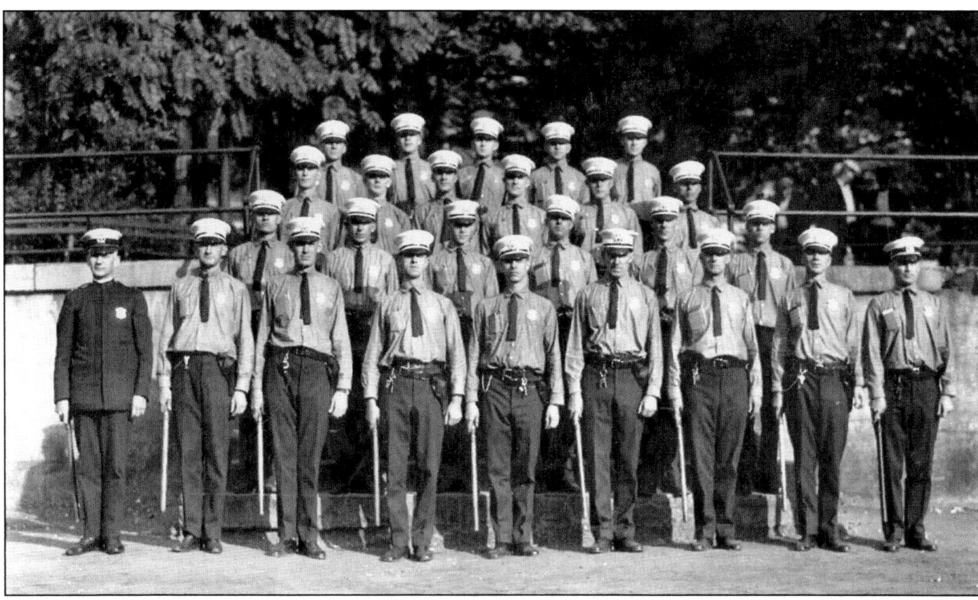

In 1927, this group of police offers was assigned to the foot traffic patrol. During Cincinnati's growth in the early 1900s, foot patrol officers were often stationed downtown to direct traffic and help with other issues. Since this was during the height of Prohibition, officers made 35,608 arrests: 3,231 for drunkenness, 3,419 for liquor possession, 228 for liquor sales, and 219 for liquor transport.

The first police recruit class is pictured in April 1927. Lt. Gustav Lorenz was the head of the School of Instruction at this time, a department that later became the Cincinnati Police Academy. Before 1927, a new officer was paired with a veteran and given very little direction for apprehending criminals or even conducting a routine patrol. Recruit regulations in 1886 suggested that patrolmen be between the age of 21 to 40 years old, and lieutenants ages 21 to 50. The minimum required height was five feet, seven inches, and recruits were tested on their power, speed, and running endurance. The beginnings of an official recruit class started in 1912, when a military organizational style was adopted and a recruit squad was organized in accordance with U.S. Army regulations. Recruit stipulations changed in 1959, when a statute deemed only high school graduates could become policemen. By the 1960s, a psychologist was incorporated into the recruiting process to develop a profile of attributes police recruits should possess.

From left to right stand George Murphy, boxing commissioner; W. C. Kellogg, city manager during the late 1920s; and Al Bechtold, boxing commissioner. As commissioners, Murphy and Bechtold were probably paid to regulate amateur boxing in the city. These trophies were won by Silver Gloves, which is thought to be a light-weight championship or a class below Golden Gloves, which is the name of a first-rate boxing tournament.

A Cincinnati patrol group stops to pose for a picture while attending a picnic for orphans in 1930 at Coney Island. The police officers are, from left to right, Thomas McCollum, John Dressing, George Karman, Edward Clott, Lt. Bart Milligan, Thomas Shearwood, Raymond McVeigh, Joseph Ploeger, and Edward Dollenmeyer. These officers were on hand to play with the children and ensure the day went smoothly.

This joyous police parade took place in the early 1930s and was captured in this picture taken on Plum Street, looking north from Sixth Street. There was a lot to celebrate during this year: a police library opened in 1932 in the basement of city hall, and a citywide safety patrol was organized in 1933. The next year the Traffic Accident Investigation Squad was established.

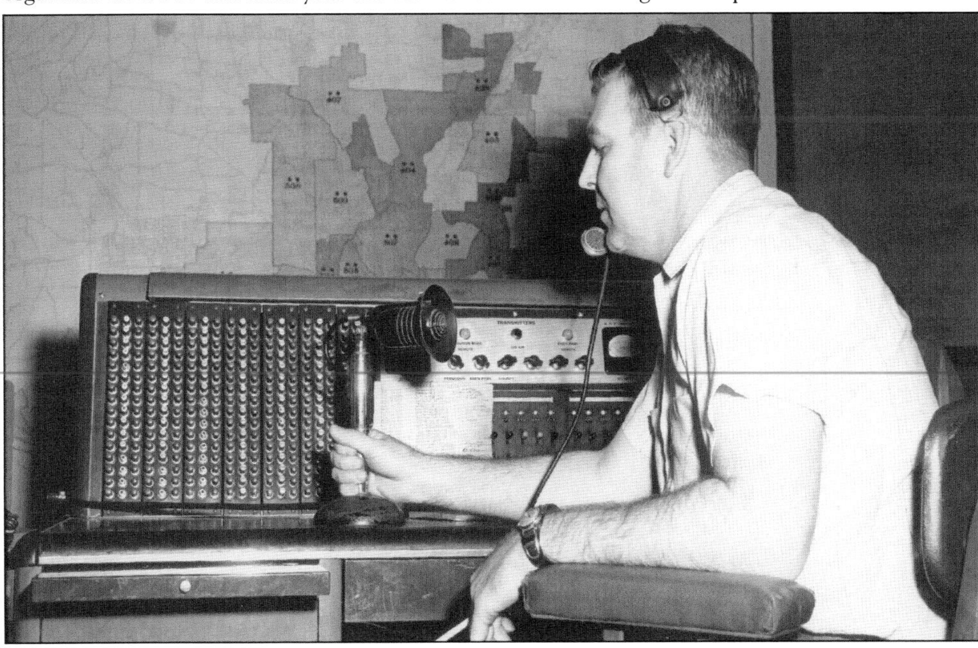

In 1930, the police retained a University of Cincinnati electrical engineering student to design, construct, and install this radio system. The system was upgraded in 1944, when a radio system was boosted to a 35-megahertz base station. At first, 10 FM mobile units were installed and, later, 35 FM mobile units were used. In 1949, the radio system was further enhanced to include a high band FM system.

This rare photograph, taken around the 1930s, shows two unique Cincinnati police officers: Patrick Whalen, on the left, was the last horse-drawn vehicle driver when this operation was discarded in 1913. Now a motorized patrol driver, Whalen stands next to another motorized car driver. Seven patrol cars were purchased in 1912 to replace the 10 horse patrols, and by the next year, all horse patrol wagons were officially retired.

Car radios were first installed in 1931 to 51 patrol cars. In 1941, a new police dispatch center opened in the Communications Building at 1430 Martin Drive and 40 police and 10 fire division two-way radios were installed in vehicles. In 1954, two-way radios were used, and in 1971, new portable radios replaced these older car radios.

On June 16, 1931, a T antenna was installed at the water works pumping station in Eden Park. With call letters WKDU, this tower held both police and fire VHF (very high frequency) antennas. Also in 1931, Station X was created with one sergeant and a radio operator based out of Central Station in city hall. In 1971, Motorola installed six channels in a UHF (ultrahigh frequency) range to further boost police communications.

Robert Klug displays accident investigation techniques, including how to take pictures of the scene with the department-issued camera of that time. Cincinnati's Traffic Accident Investigation Squad was officially established in 1934 and was equipped with cameras, measuring tape, road flares, first aid kits, and more necessary supplies in 1936. At that time, more than 600 officers worked on the force.

Sitting here are, from left to right, William Duritsch, Lonnie Neimeister, and Irvin Diehl. Born on March 18, 1912, Neimeister joined the department on March 22, 1937. He worked in Districts 4 and 5, was an instructor at the target range, and worked in the Motorcycle Department from 1960 to 1968. In his career, he was one of the top marksmen in the CPD.

Taken during the 1937 flood, this picture shows the Cincinnati police helping out those who lived in the neighboring city of Middletown during this intrusive, countywide flood. Since many surrounding villages and towns had few resources to sustain their own police force, Cincinnati officers often helped out during emergencies or for other, smaller matters whenever necessary.

Patrolman Bob Sherwood was a member of the 1937 police recruit class, along with Jack O'Hare, William Means, Ed Cavanaugh, John Wellen, Tony Schir, Bill Donovan, Bill Klosterman, Charlie Davis, Bob Arthur, Pat Daugherty, Roger Lammers, Melvin Pell, Paul Wuellner, Ray Handley, and Lawrence Kloster (although none of the men are identified in the picture). At this time, Gustav Lorenz was still in charge of the police academy.

George Albert Plum worked on the force for 24 years. Known as "Big George," he patrolled Districts 7, 2, and 4, and was on foot patrol. He later became a turnkey (a jailor at the basement jail in Central Station). His son George C. Plum also served as a Cincinnati patrolman prior to a stint in the army during World War II.

These traffic officers are, from left to right, Ray Pratt, Jerry Thomas, and Lonnie Neimeister. Pratt and his first wife, Dot, are noted for being the first husband and wife to be president of the local Fraternal Order of Police (FOP) lodge and president of the ladies auxiliary, respectively, at the same time. Pratt worked as a guard at the Cincinnati Workhouse in 1941 and entered the police department on July 1, 1942, and worked at Districts 4 and 5.

Lee Flaugher, shown here in his early days as an officer, retired from the police on May 1, 1941. Flaugher was a horse patrolman for an early police district that covered the O'Bryonville-Oakley-Madisonville area and later became the first detective assigned to the Cincinnati Vice Squad. He spent his retirement on a farm he bought in Oregonia, Ohio.

The Cincinnati police tug-of-war team poses for a picture around 1940. Seen here are (first row, kneeling) officers Fred Zobel, Paul Steurer, McCarthy, Beverly Thomas, Robert Brumfield, and Frank Acito; (second row, standing) officers Lambert, George Bonkowski, Charles Martin, Lt. George Schattle, Iwanski, Erhardt Erdman, and Paul Bare. Schattle was the second-best graduate in his recruit class, after Lieutenant Colonel York (the first) and before Sgt. William Kipp (the third). Erdman was a member of the 1937 police class, as well as Paul Steurer, Beverly Thomas, Pete Barber, and Harvey Schaedle. Fred Zobel joined the department on June 1, 1935, and was assigned to District 1. His salary at that time was $1,500 per year. On September 21, 1942, he took a leave from the department to enlist in the U.S. Army. He retired March 23, 1963, after serving more than 27 years. Zobel was also a charter member of the Queen City Lodge and served as secretary from 1946 to 1947. In 1951, he was promoted to sergeant and his pay increased to $7,000. Brumfield entered the police department on June 14, 1937, and worked in Districts 4 and 3. He retired in 1966.

Taken around 1942 at District 3, these patrolmen stand outside the patrol 5 wagon. The first seven patrol wagons were purchased in 1912 to replace the 10 horse patrols. By 1924, horses were completely replaced by vehicles, and coupes were introduced in 1928. That same year, the force was completely motorized. Sirens and special speedometers were installed in 21 vehicles in 1938, and blow-out proof tires were installed the next year.

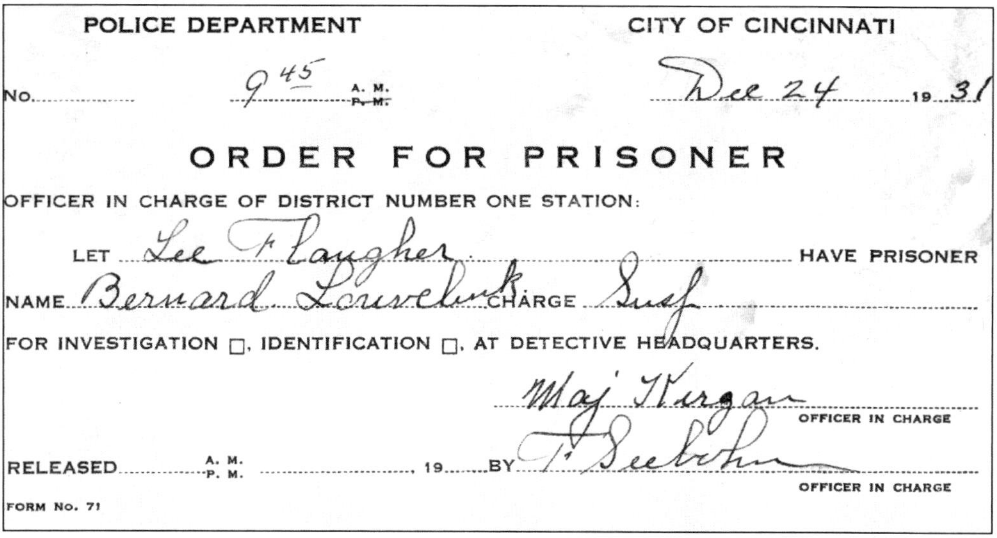

POLICE DEPARTMENT CITY OF CINCINNATI

NO. 9 45 A. M. Dec 24 1931

ORDER FOR PRISONER

OFFICER IN CHARGE OF DISTRICT NUMBER ONE STATION:

LET Lee F Flaugher HAVE PRISONER

NAME Bernard Louvelink CHARGE Susf

FOR INVESTIGATION ☐, IDENTIFICATION ☐, AT DETECTIVE HEADQUARTERS.

Maj Kirgan OFFICER IN CHARGE

RELEASED A. M. P. M. 19 BY F. Seebohn OFFICER IN CHARGE

FORM No. 71

Donated by Lee Flaugher, this slip of paper decries that Flaugher has the authority to move his prisoner from one location to another (perhaps from a holding cell to the court). Col. William Copelan was in charge of the police force at this time, a position he held from 1912 to 1935.

In 1938, traffic officers gather for a group shot during an Auto Accident Reconstruction class. In 1955, the Traffic Bureau moved to headquarters at 310 Lincoln Park Drive, sharing the building with the Juvenile Bureau and District 1. In the late 1960s, the Traffic Bureau got some much-needed equipment when two cameras were purchased for cars assigned exclusively to the expressway patrol.

Taken on November 4, 1938, a prisoner stands near a paddy wagon. In those days, the police would hold the offenders in a small jail at their district. Then city hall sent out a paddy wagon to pick up the prisoner for transport to Central Station, a jail in the city hall basement. The prisoner was tried in court on the first floor of city hall and, if found guilty, sent to the workhouse on Colerain Avenue.

Henry Sandman first joined the park police as a patrolman on May 18, 1940. He became a Cincinnati police recruit in November of that year, and was assigned to District 2 as a patrolman on February 1, 1941. Throughout the 1940s, he worked on Race Relations detail, the Youth Aid Bureau, the Traffic Bureau, and the Crime Bureau. On March 15, 1965, Sandman was appointed to safety director for the city. In June 1975, he was further promoted to deputy city manager for Cincinnati, a job he held until June 25, 1977. Again, the next day, Sandman transferred to a new job as the director of safety at the University of Cincinnati. Two years later, 11 Cincinnatians were killed in a rush to obtain festival seating at a 1979 Who concert. A few days after the concert, Sandman headed a crowd safety task force to study and develop increased safety measures for festival seating.

Taken in 1941, this picture shows the beginning process of booking a prisoner. When found guilty, prisoners were taken to the first floor of city hall. Here they were fingerprinted, photographed, and their height and weight was recorded. The first floor was home to much police activity in these days; the police chief's office was here, as well as Detective Headquarters and the Traffic Unit.

These policemen stand up straight for roll call in 1942, possibly taken in the District 2 police station. That year, police officers were able to use urinalysis in cases of drivers or accident victims suspected under the influence of alcohol. Just a year before, the FOP, Queen City Lodge No. 69, was established—a move that encouraged increased comradery among officers.

Guy P. Smallwood, a member of the Cincinnati park police, stands in front of his patrol car on January 8, 1942. The park police started around 1891 or 1892 as a force separate from the CPD. The city decided such a department was needed to protect the city's parks, since Cincinnati police already had their hands full with activities going on in the city. Park policemen had the same powers that city policemen had, and the two groups assisted each other when necessary. The park police merged with the Cincinnati police in 1989. Smallwood's son, Roger, was born around 1946 and joined the Cincinnati police force around 1964, the same year the district boundaries were realigned to equitably distribute the work among seven districts. Roger retired on July 13, 1996, after more than 30 years of working with the city.

In April 1942, five men stopped from their daily duties at District 2 to pose for a picture. These men are, from left to right, Sgt. Lloyd Simmion, Lt. George Dooley, Capt. Mack Hall, Lt. Walter Martin, and Sgt. Bob Welz. Welz joined the police department on August 1, 1934, and attended recruit school when it was held in the basement of city hall. He was assigned to District 4 and served six years there. In January 1940, he was promoted to detective and became sergeant on August 5 of that year. He continued to advance his career and retired on June 18, 1968, as chief of detectives of the Cincinnati Crime Bureau. Two years prior to his retirement, he fell while cleaning his gutters, and broke both his arms. As fate would have it, his son Bob Jr. was also admitted to the hospital for back problems. Father and son stayed in the same room, so Bob Sr. acted as Bob Jr.'s legs, and Bob Jr. acted as Bob Sr.'s arms.

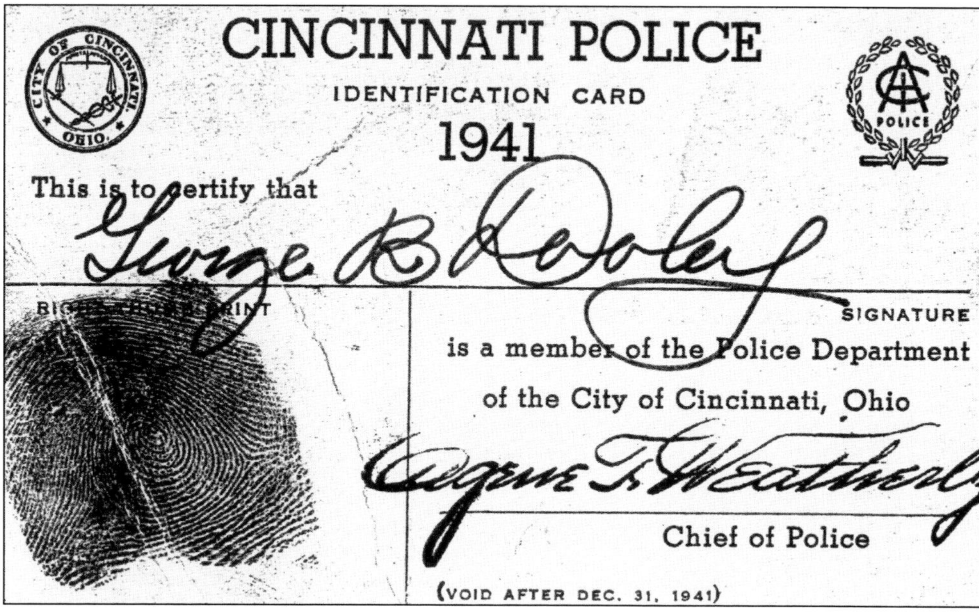

CINCINNATI POLICE
IDENTIFICATION CARD
1941

This is to certify that George B. Dooley

RIGHT THUMB PRINT

SIGNATURE

is a member of the Police Department of the City of Cincinnati, Ohio

Eugene T. Weatherly

Chief of Police

(VOID AFTER DEC. 31, 1941)

George B. Dooley's identification card in 1941 belies the officer's 28 years on the force. Born in 1891 and appointed as patrolman on November 28, 1913, Dooley was promoted to sergeant in 1925 and lieutenant in 1928. Throughout his career, Dooley worked at District 7, District 4, Headquarters (District 1), and District 2.

The City of Cincinnati, Ohio

To all to whom these Presents shall come, Greeting:

KNOW YE *that the City Manager of the City of Cincinnati, Ohio, by virtue of the authority vested in him by the provisions of* The General Code of Ohio *and in accordance with the* Certificate of the Civil Service Commissioners *of said city,* does hereby appoint George B. Dooley a Police Captain *in the* Police *Force of the City of Cincinnati, and he is hereby authorized and empowered, during his good behavior to execute and discharge all and singular the duties appertaining to said office, and to enjoy all the privileges and immunities thereof.*

In Testimony Whereof, *I have hereunto set my hand and caused the seal of the City of Cincinnati, Ohio to be affixed this* 15th *day of* December, 1941

City Manager

Dooley was promoted to captain after the death of Maj. Charles Easton (the title of major was changed to captain). A few years later, Dooley was killed in 1943 while attempting to arrest Jesse Anderson at 519 West Fifth Street. Anderson shot Dooley through the chest. Dooley was 50 years old at the time, making him the highest-ranking officer to be killed in duty.

Detective Jack Huber (left) and Paul Schirmer study evidence, possibly at the first crime lab in Cincinnati, which was stationed at General Hospital and later moved to city hall. Huber joined the department on October 1, 1941, and was first assigned to District 5. On the same day 10 years later, Huber joined the Detective Headquarters as a newly promoted detective and worked with John "Slim" Bugganer on many tough cases. He transferred to the Homicide Department in 1954, a department he stayed at until his retirement in 1968. Teamed with Tom Faragher, Huber worked on many highly publicized and nationally known murder cases in Cincinnati, including the Audrey Pugh case, the detective Walter Hart murder, the Rape-Strangulation Slayings, patrolman Donald Martin's murder, and many more. After Huber retired, he worked for the Wackenhut Corporation as area manager and stayed with them until 1973. He then worked for Russ Poland in the Hamilton County Municipal Court bailiff's office and remained there until 1978. After this, he did some part-time private investigative work for several agencies before retiring completely.

On February 9, 1942, the Identification Bureau took this print of citizens paying their car fees or traffic tickets on the second floor of city hall. Just two years earlier, the Identification Bureau installed the Battley single-fingerprint file system, and in 1941, a Century police camera was purchased. In 1943, they upgraded to a Speed Graphic camera, and other accessories were purchased to make photographing fingerprints at crime scenes easier.

The 1943 recruit class poses for their picture outside city hall. Notice the men standing in military uniforms on the back edges of the picture. They are either police recruits that had been drafted into the military and returned to be photographed in their recruit class picture or military officers brought in to train Cincinnati officers on World War II technology.

The Police Safety Swing Band originated in 1946 thanks to the efforts of John Turigliatto. The musicians in this picture are, from left to right, officers Eurkamp, Smith, Simmons, Robert Lipka, Gick, Robert Shearwood, Liebel, Hicks, Rellar, Schira, and Wheat. They toured all over the city, encouraging citizens to follow basic safety laws while driving and in other situations.

Detective Frederick Seebohm was killed in the line of duty in 1947 when his motorcycle crashed into a motorbus in Northside. Frederick was a brother to Maj. John Seebohm, a respected officer who placed the last call from the police and fire call boxes. In 1971, John, at the time a retired officer, dressed up in his old uniform and made one final call to city hall before the last call box was removed.

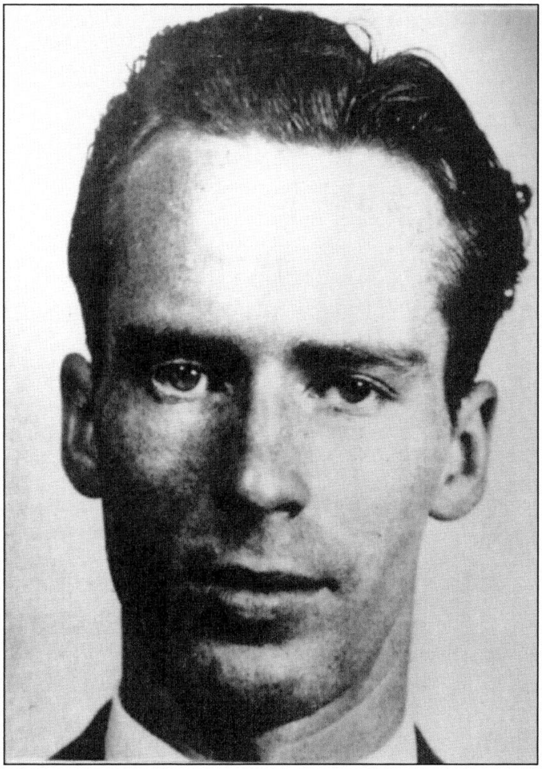

Patrolman John W. Hughes was appointed a police officer on February 1, 1943, and died On June 19, 1948. On that day, Hughes was driving his motorcycle down Kellogg Avenue and chasing after a speeding violator when he collided with a taxi. He died from injuries suffered in that accident.

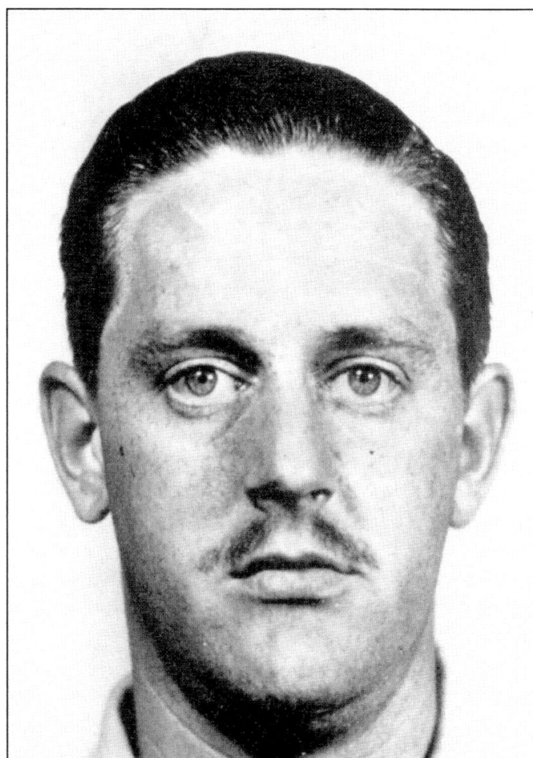

Patrolman Lewis William Hall was also killed in the line of duty while chasing a speeding violator. In November 1948, Hall was chasing a speeder down Queen City Avenue when his motorcycle hit something in the road. This bump diverted him off the road, and he later died from injuries suffered as a result of that motorcycle accident.

Cincinnati police and friends celebrate a Memorial Day remembrance in 1939 by playing songs, reading the officers killed in the line of duty, listening to speeches, and more. During this era, the annual police celebration was held in either the Taft or Emory Auditoriums. In 2007, the police celebrated Memorial Day by marching to the police memorial on Ezzard Charles Drive and listening to speeches and singing songs.

On October 15, 1950, officers and their families celebrated the dedication of District 6 on 3295 Erie Avenue in East Hyde Park. Built in 1899 at 3855 Eastern Avenue, District 6 opened temporary at Delta Avenue and Columbia Parkway in 1948, until this grand opening. In 2007, this district continues to operate as District 2.

Eugene T. Weatherly, shown here on the left, joined the force on January 29, 1908. He was known for often reaching out to help the children in his community; on May 6, 1940, he took 750 members of the Ninth Street boys club to the circus. He was also well-respected on the force.

Weatherly worked his way up to inspector, which he officially became on June 5, 1925, and became the assistant Cincinnati chief of police on January 1, 1928, and the acting chief on December 1, 1934. Just a few months later, on February 1, 1935, he was appointed chief of police.

Weatherly officially retired on March 1, 1950. For his going-away party, where this picture was taken, the police corps hosted a testimonial dinner for him at the Netherland Plaza's Hall of Mirrors. This festivity was held on Wednesday, February 15, 1950, at 6:30 p.m. At the time of his retirement, Weatherly's title had changed again to police chief, a position he was appointed to on October 16, 1941.

Retirement did not set well with Weatherly, who is shown here at his retirement party. Forced to take it easy because of a heart ailment, Weatherly became increasingly distressed with his life off the force. On February 20, 1953, at age 72, he took his own life. He left behind two sons, Joseph and Eugene Jr., and a step-son, Milo Hanke. His first wife, Mary Looker Hanke, died in 1944.

John Turigliatto was a musician at heart. Growing up in Braidwood, Illinois, he and his friends started a band called the Illinois Aces. Before joining the police department as a substitute patrolman in 1927, he worked for six years as a firefighter and started the fire department's marching band. When he became a police officer, he started the police department's drum and bugle corps. While he led the police marching band, he was also instrumental in creating the swing band. Five instrumentalists and one vocalist performed at movie houses and for teen groups. They boasted 50 appearances their first year. Besides being a wonderful musician and teacher, Turigliatto is also known for starting the Crime Prevention Bureau in 1943, a department he became the commander of on August 16, 1945. This bureau's name later changed to the Youth Aid Bureau and served the needs of abused or neglected area children. Turigliatto retired on May 1, 1952.

The *Play It Safe* program aired on WCPO-Channel 9 and was sponsored by the FOP. Taken on September 23, 1950, this picture shows Capt. Ray Clift and Sgt. Charles Martin as guest speakers. Turigliatto started the *Play it Safe* show in the 1930s, and it was so popular in 1953, that the concept was brought to elementary schools as well. *Police Call*, another WCPO television show, aired from 1968 to 1982.

Turigliatto lets on how much fun he is having leading the police marching band. Police chief Eugene Weatherly enjoyed the band so much that he would not sign a parade permit if Turigliatto's band did not lead the parade. Turigliatto also organized annual musical tributes for deceased police officers—these programs were performed at Taft Auditorium.

Patrolman Walter H. Williams joined the force on July 1, 1950, and was killed in the line of duty on October 17, 1951. At 2:30 a.m. that morning, Williams was driving west on Laidlaw Avenue when he collided with a 1951 Ford Sedan northbound on Paddock Road in District 7. Williams suffered a possible skull fracture and broken neck.

In 1952, the Police Training School was renamed the Police Academy, and it moved from city hall to the second floor of the District 2 building at 314 Broadway, where this picture was taken. In 1996, a Student Police Academy was established to teach middle school students about local law enforcement, and 75 students received certificates of completion that first year. The school continues to operate today.

Three

ADVANCES IN THE FORCE 1952–1976

Dale Derbyshire sits on his 1947 Harley Davidson for a picture taken in 1952. Derbyshire joined the force February 15, 1951, and served for 30 years, mostly in the motorcycle division. During his tenure, there were very few uniform regulations, especially for motorcycle officers. Some wore Western-style gun holders, and others carried different guns than the ones issued to them by the department.

George O'Reilley Jr. sits on his 1953 Harley Davidson motorcycle. His father, George O'Reilley Sr., joined the force in 1929 and drove a three-wheeler in District 5. George Sr. retired in 1955, just four years after his son joined the force. George Jr. also worked on motorcycle patrol; he retired in 1979. George Jr.'s son, George Allen O'Reilley, was on the force from 1966 to 1996.

Cooperation from citizens is essential to an effective police service. In this picture, police chief Stanley R. Schrotel, on the left, presents an appreciation award to president Frank J. VanLahr and employees of the Walnut Hills Provident Bank for assistance in apprehending two bank robbers. The thieves attempted to steal $4,000. Although this exact date is not known, it must be between 1951 and 1967, during Schrotel's tenure as police chief.

Officers take notes on a staged vehicular accident on Fourth Street, downtown Cincinnati. Taken around 1953, this picture shows a Ford police car and a Plymouth in a head-to-head accident, and a group of new officers recording their preliminary notes on the accident. Through these types of examples, officers quickly learn how to investigate car accidents in the field.

Patrolman Robert V. Bastin was appointed on April 15, 1951, and died on March 7, 1953. At 1:35 a.m. that day, he collided with a car heading south on John Street, driven by 35-year-old David Hines. Bastin was fatally injured and pronounced dead at 2:17 a.m. Hines was arrested and charged with driving under the influence and reckless driving.

Clem Merz Jr. crouches in the first row of this picture on the far left. Officers Jacob Schott and Leslie Thompson sit in the second row (the second and third officers from the right). In the third row stands, from left to right, an unidentified officer, Robert Meldon, Robert Welz, Ben Shaffer, George Ebbers, and two unidentified men. This picture was probably taken at the old FOP hall on Eastern Avenue in the late 1950s. Schott started with the force in 1937 and worked his way up to police chief in 1967. He helped develop inspection procedures and the *Standard Operational Procedures* manual. Meldon joined on February 1, 1936, and retired in 1964; Welz worked from 1934 to 1968. Thompson worked from 1927 to 1960 and was known for being very dependable. Ebbers joined the force in 1951 and retired in 1977.

Police officer Charlie Davidson, on the left, demonstrates first aid practices. This photograph was taken to promote a new police medical unit being put into place in the 1950s. This was also the year "scout cars" were introduced. The police used these cars to transport citizens with minor injuries and pregnant women to the hospital or dead bodies from a crime scene to the morgue. The police took on this role from the beginning of the force up until the 1980s, when the fire department took over such duties. Scout cars began because of the death of J. Roy Hicks, who died in the line of duty on February 25, 1935, just eight days after he played the bugle at the third annual police memorial services. When he died in the field, officers did not have the means to take him to the hospital for at least 30 minutes. So Cincinnati bought seven new "Combination Cruiser/Invalid Cars." Nicknamed scout cars, each was equipped with two stretchers and first aid kits. In 2007, the police still use scout cars, though not as often.

The police motorcyclists in this picture are, from left to right, A. U. Thiel, Gene Nobel, Bill Duritsch, Bill Cappel, John McElhaney, Carl Poppe, Bill Finnell, Dale Derbyshire, Bill "Big Stoop" Klosterman, Charlie Black, Wayne Waite, and Nolan Bradley. It is believed that Bradley was the first African American motorcycle officer. This picture was taken in 1952 outside of city hall. Klosterman was a member of the 1937 police class, along with Bradley. Klosterman joined the motorcycle group in July 1942 and stayed in the highway safety patrol until August 4, 1965. Cappel joined the force years later in 1941, and was immediately assigned to "Old Bloody Four," the fourth police district. In 1943, he enlisted in the navy, and he returned to District 4 as soon as he was released from the navy in February 1946. He was assigned to motorcycles in May 1947. After six years, he switched to speed control cars.

Walter T. Hart joined the force May 1, 1929, and died in the line of duty on September 19, 1955. On that day, Hart was dining at the Grey Eagle Café when Lemuel Trotter, Robert Lee Jackson, and Willie Barnet attempted a robbery. A shoot-out ensued, and Walter, a 20-year-veteran homicide detective, was shot in the heart. He tried to call for help but died before he got the chance.

Bicycle inspections were held around the city to make sure kids' and adults' bikes were in working order. This photograph, taken on August 19, 1957, at a park in Bond Hill, shows officer Robert Shearwood with a group of children. Officers also put stickers on the bikes with numbers that corresponded to records held at the police station in case a bike was lost or stolen.

This recruit class graduated on December 24, 1956. Class members included Lt. Elmer Ries, Wes Mysonheimer, Sgt. Stan Carle (Carle originally joined the force on February 1, 1939), Jim Dettone, Clyde English, Gus Feldman, Don Freese, Dale Gadberry, Walt Lischer, George Rosen, Frank Sefton, Charlie Watkins, Don Omer (who later became the Delhi fire chief), Jerome Schimpf (who became a key member in solving police officer Don Martin's murder), and Jerome Zwick. In the fourth row are three Amerbley Village policemen (Paul Freeland, on the left, later transferred to the CPD), two new St. Bernard recruits, and five Cincinnati police cadets, Jerry Andres, Ken Oden, Max Lettrell, Joe Stoeckel, and William Vogel.

Police officers Capt. Walter Martin (on the left) and Lt. Col. Guy York (on the right) stand with city manager C. O. Harrell. On December 8, 1957, these three men paused for a picture during the dedication ceremony of the new District 5 station at 1012 Ludlow Avenue near Central Parkway.

Officer Roger Herron stands with his wife officer Patricia Whalen. Whalen was the only one of 13 women to pass the 1958 police civil service exam. She started recruit school on November 17 of that year and shocked her male coworkers and superiors by requesting to take the civil service exam in 1963. Before her, there was not even an official uniform for women, so Whalen made her own.

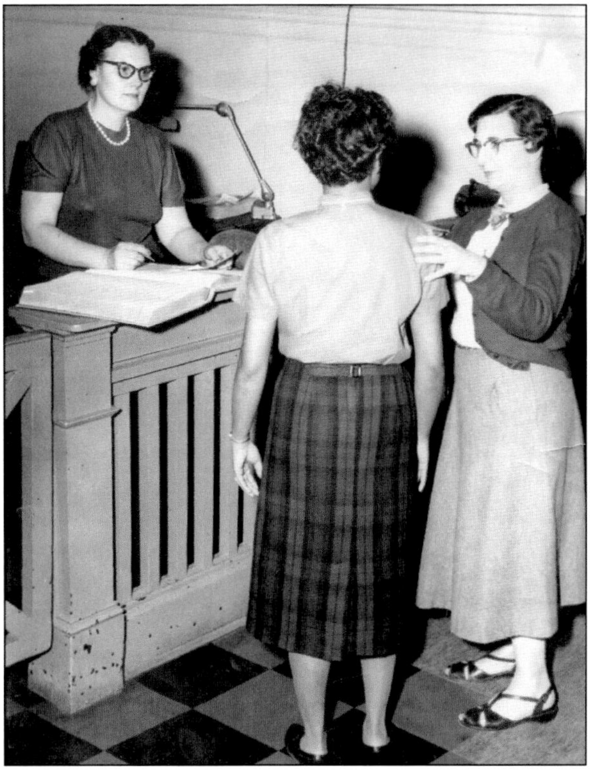

In January 1958, Lois Crabtree, the police matron, demonstrates how she checks in female detainees. The records clerk at that time stands in the center next to Betty Altmeyer. The women's detention center started out on the top floor of city hall, but in 1930, the center moved to the bottom floor.

The records clerk stands on the left, as police matron Crabtree points to the rights allowed each perpetrator. This picture was also taken in January 1958, the same year old mechanical sirens in patrol cars began to be replaced by modern electronic sirens. Now, officers could use their sirens as public address systems or to direct officers while away from their cars.

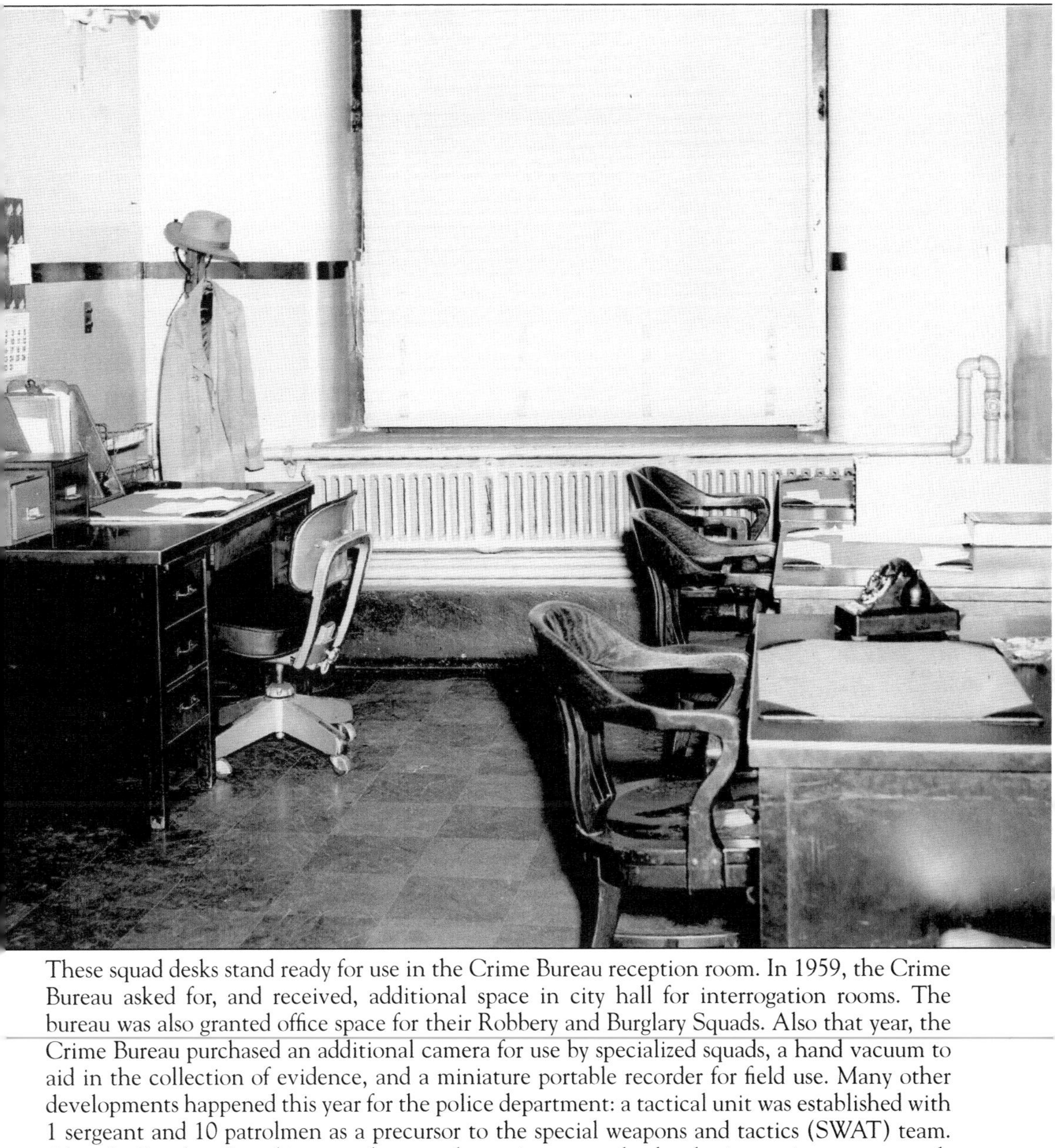

These squad desks stand ready for use in the Crime Bureau reception room. In 1959, the Crime Bureau asked for, and received, additional space in city hall for interrogation rooms. The bureau was also granted office space for their Robbery and Burglary Squads. Also that year, the Crime Bureau purchased an additional camera for use by specialized squads, a hand vacuum to aid in the collection of evidence, and a miniature portable recorder for field use. Many other developments happened this year for the police department: a tactical unit was established with 1 sergeant and 10 patrolmen as a precursor to the special weapons and tactics (SWAT) team. Also, the Burglary Squad improved protocols at crime scenes by developing a crime scene search kit. Newly passed state legislation also ensured that all future applicants to the police division must be high school graduates.

In 1958, Lt. Arthur Mehring became the first helicopter traffic officer. He and his pilot, Jack DeVise, patrolled from the air for one hour each morning and one hour each afternoon. Bill Beahr was the last helicopter policeman to patrol the skies; this job is now handled by private companies.

Taken at District 6 on Erie Avenue, patrolman Robert Sharhag is holding a police receiver. Used in the 1960s, this early technology was not quite a two-way device yet. Sharhag is also holding his nightstick in the traditional way; although officers had a belt ring to hold the stick, it was uncomfortable and difficult to use in an emergency. For improved comfort and access, officers carried the sticks under their arms.

Taken in the city hall basement jail, this picture shows the fine facilities enjoyed by inmates. Although Central Station jail is no longer there, a stone-carved police badge is still displayed on city hall, representing the police's long history with city hall. The city hall courtyard used to be such a key part of the force's activities that a gas pump was installed solely for police cars.

This "Notice of Arrest" police notebook, referred to as No. 314, was used by Cincinnati officers for any type of "notice to appear." The form 314, also known as the "NTA" or "Notice to Appear," is still used today, in only slightly different form. When an officer writes a ticket, the white copy goes to the courts, the yellow goes to the citizen, and the police officer keeps the blue copy.

Police officer Mike Parker works with canine officer Ringo. The Canine Unit was first deployed on patrol in July 1961 after completion of a 15-week training course. The Canine Unit did, and continues today, train at the target range at 10139 Sparten Drive in the Evendale/Lincoln Heights area.

Officers show off the abilities of their canine partners at a canine ability demonstration downtown at Fifth and Walnut Streets, right on Fountain Square. Patrolman Thomas Harvey and his two dogs, Smokey and Arno, were part of the inaugural group of canine officers. Sgt. George McNair was their supervisor during these first days.

Police officer Thomas Harvey stands on the left, and officer Jim Royer (who at this time was the president of the FOP) stands on the right. In the Canine Unit's inaugural year, the squad used four new compact station wagons to transport both dogs and officers. Also the troops were assigned portable transistor receivers and two-frequency radios.

Patrick Olvey stands by a police badge display he set up in 1967 at District 7 for an open house. Olvey has a large personal collection of badges and often takes them on the road to display at other police stations. Olvey worked on the CPD from January 14, 1963, to February 22, 1992. As of 2007, he is the president and historian of the Greater Cincinnati Police Historical Society.

Donald Martin was appointed to the force on April 30, 1956, and died March 11, 1961. His murder was not solved until 2005, when two homicide detectives, Kurt Ballman and Jeff Schare, reopened the case. They deducted that on that day, Walter Walls, Jesse Walls, and Charles Jillson entered a car lot at 715 Reading Road to steal a car battery. The Wallses entered the lot on foot while Jillson waited in the car. Martin pulled his patrol car into a parking lot at 721 Reading Road around 3:00 a.m., walked onto the car lot, and caught Walter tampering with a vehicle. A violent struggle ensued and Walter, possibly with Jesse's assistance, gained control of Martin's .38 caliber service revolver and shot Martin in the chest. Martin ran, and Walter shot him again in the back. At 3:10 a.m., Jack Wenner, Hugh Moore, and Harold Stiver happened to be driving by and observed the shooting. Walter ran away, discarding Martin's gun. Stiver exited the witness vehicle and assisted Martin while the others called the police. Martin died, and the offenders escaped.

Constance Breitbeil practices self-defense in classes at the YMCA on Central Parkway. Breitbeil joined the force on March 30 1964, and was assigned to the Youth Aid Section. She left the force on February 15, 1968. At this time, women on the force worked out with men, becoming judo experts like all officers. The push for women to be on the force started in 1912, when the Women's Taxpayers' League petitioned then-mayor Hunt to assign a woman to the police force to watch over women and children in the city. They asked that this task be assigned to Sarah Falconer, a former jail matron. Many years later, Mary Therese Mechley and Elissa McArthur became the first woman to be hired as uniformed police officers, meaning that they went right to work on the streets as beat officers. They were both sworn in during September 1974.

Constance Breitbeil practices her fighting technique with fellow police officer Don Davis. Both are members of the No. 42 recruit class, which graduated from the police academy in 1964. Recruit Robert Colonel stands to the left of the picture, with his hands up, and Robert Schaust stands on the far right of the picture.

Two members of the Cincinnati Motorcycle Squad, including Mel Thurman on the left, and an unidentified officer on the right, pose with area kids. This picture was probably taken during safety week at District 1 during the 1960s. Motorcycles were first introduced to the squad around 1911–1913. In 1939, four three-wheeled motorcycles (which is what Thurman is driving) were purchased for downtown parking enforcement.

Young police cadets stand for a class picture in June 1966. In the picture stands, from left to right, (first row) graduates A. Comose, R. Kaegle, M. Snowden, and J. Simon; (second row) R. Disbennett, K. Kemper, Richardson, Brown, R. Burger, and C. Kreimer. Col. Michael C. Snowden rose through the ranks of the CPD and was eventually promoted to police chief in 1992. As the 30th leader of the force, Snowden served in this position until 1998. A police cadet classification was established on June 20, 1955, the same year the department started using polygraph tests, and in 1963, a police science program started at the University of Cincinnati. In 1967, the cadet program advanced, and cadets began working as co-op students—they alternated between working on the force and attending college classes. More recently, a Citizens Police Academy was established in 1994.

Sgt. Albert F. Weller served on the CPD from June 14, 1937, until his death on August 6, 1967. Weller helped quell a riot on the *Jubilee* river boat at the public landing, and then suffered a massive heart attack afterwards. He left behind a wife, Virginia, and a sister, Ruth—one of the first four police women to join the Cincinnati police force.

The Holy Name Society is a group of Catholic police officers. In this picture are, from left to right, (first row) Earl Gaynor and James Kiefer; (second row) Thomas Bowns and Thomas Stegmoyer. All four men served at the 18th annual police Holy Name Society Communion Mass. Al Stephen, then athletic director of Xavier University, was the guest speaker.

Hamilton County deputy sheriffs stand guard during the 1967 Cincinnati riots. The second largest civil rights demonstration in the city's history, these devastating riots started on June 12, 1967, in minority neighborhoods that alleged police abuse and deteriorating living conditions. The Cincinnati police called on the Ohio National Guard and the Hamilton County deputy sheriffs to help calm rioters; 1 death and 404 arrests were reported. After this incident, the Mutual Aid Act was established, encouraging the Cincinnati and Hamilton County departments to work together when needed, including the sharing of personnel, equipment, and other resources. Riots again exploded in Cincinnati in April 1968, after the assassination of civil rights leader Martin Luther King Jr. Some factors that led to this riot, as reported in 1968 by the Commission on Civil Disorders, were segregated neighborhoods and police officers' bias against minorities.

The 49th recruit class of patrolmen attended recruit school from November 20, 1967, to February 23, 1968. They are, from left to right, (first row) Calvin Long, James Reeves, Thomas Weilbacher, Edward Woodyard, Sgt. Norman Hughes, Lt. Robert Heinlein, Sgt. Robert Johnson, Jack Merritt, Edward Collins, Robert Smith, Robert Mradigan (Greenhills patrol) and H. Bruce Knox; (second row) Donald Ruberg, Rodney Carr, Robert Hungler, William Lindemann, William Edwards, Richard Schmalz, Ralph Gosser, William Mackay, Bruce Sillett, Jack Gates, Jack Sommer, and an unidentified officer; (third row) Kenneth Ottlinger, Dennis Schlie (patrol for Indian hill), Kenneth Lawson, Ivan Singleton, Ronald McConn, Paul Lotc, Richard Duell, Kurtis Lyons, Bert Blair, George Hough (patrol for Reading), Vernon Smith, and Thomas Mehas; (fourth row) Mark Hehman, Alan Cruse, Edward Rowley, Gary Bitner, Walter Wilkerson (patrol for Amberly Village), Arthur Evans, Gary Fritsch, Ronald Camden, and Lawrence Panno.

Here are, from left to right, Helen Seiler, Ruth Dagenhart, Garvey Sanders, Paul Assum, and Louise Shelley; with Capt. Charles Greer sitting. Seiler joined the force on September 1, 1947, and worked for the Youth Aid Section. She served until January 1961. Shelley, also nicknamed Lu, joined the force on March 27, 1966, and worked in the Youth Aid Section for three and a half years, then transferred to the University of Cincinnati Police Department.

Handy Matthews worked on the Vice Squad before becoming a school resource officer. This program started in October 1967 to provide service to 96 public and 60 parochial schools in the city. Matthews also initiated an early recruitment program to bring more African American officers to the CPD and later taught a criminal justice course at the University of Cincinnati.

Virginia Coffey hosts a police community relations class for new recruits at the police academy on February 19, 1968. At that time, the academy stood at 314 Broadway. Coffey was an influential civil rights leader in Cincinnati throughout the 1900s. Her resume includes organizing the first Girl Scout troop for African American girls, working as executive director of the West End branch of the YWCA in 1932, deputy director of the Mayor's Friendly Relations Committee in 1948, community relations supervisor for Seven Hills Neighborhood Houses from 1962 to 1965, and the first African American executive director of the Cincinnati Human Relations Commission, which she headed from 1968 to December 31, 1973. For her continued efforts to remove racial restrictions in restaurants, businesses, and public facilities, she received the Governor's Award for Community Action in 1973, the Good Neighbor Award in 1989, and the Great Living Cincinnatian Award in 1993.

Sgt. Milton Dills (left), Mayor Theodore M. Berry (right), and an unknown civilian pose for a photograph during Crime Prevention Week. The Crime Prevention Bureau was reestablished in 1969, along with the community relations and juvenile departments. Berry was Cincinnati's first African American mayor, and he served from December 1972 to November 1975.

The criminalistics lab stood in the basement of city hall. By 1969, all police operations moved out of the west wing of city hall, except the detention center. This movement did include criminalistics, the police gym, Motorcycle and Traffic Bureaus, and Cincinnati's police court. In 1937, indoor target ranges on the third floor and in the basement had moved to Bald Knob in Western Hills.

Tom Otten, in front, rides with Terry Meiners in 1972. These smaller motorcycles were used to patrol the downtown area. Otten's older brother Charlie was also on the force. As orphans, both brothers were raised at the Greater Cincinnati Protestant Orphanage on Beechmont Street. Before joining the department in 1954 or 1955, Charlie was part of the U.S. Marine division involved in the Chosin Reservoir battle during the Korean War.

Taken in old District 4 at 7019 Vine Street around 1970, these officers line up for a roll call. They are, from left to right, two unidentified, Eugene MacDonald, Steve Truss, Tom Bepler, Ted Fritz, and Ernie McCalla. Detectives often participate in these roll calls to discuss ongoing cases and police issues. This building still stands as a center for Hispanics.

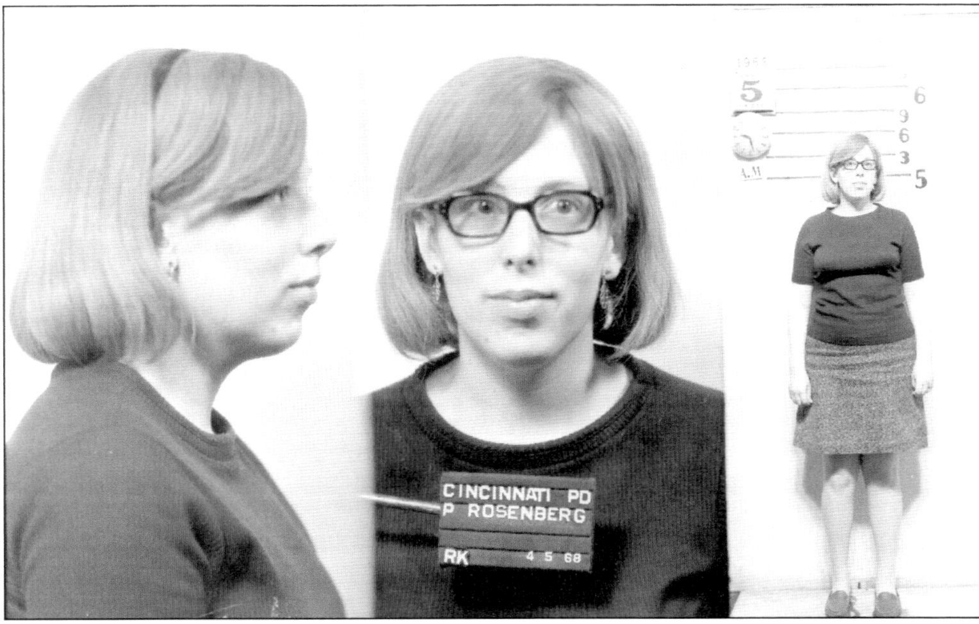

Phyllis Caskey smiles for her police recruit picture. Caskey was the first female cadet in 1968, and in 1971, she graduated with the 55th recruit class. She was assigned to the Juvenile Aid Department, as all women were during this time. But Caskey kept breaking barriers: she became a specialist in 1974, sergeant in 1981, lieutenant in 1986, and the first female district captain in 1991, overseeing District 5.

The 55th recruit class trained from March 1 to June 25, 1971. Caskey sits on the far left, and Paula J. Wagner on the right. At this time, women needed two years of college or a practical nursing degree before applying to the force, whereas men only needed a GED. But by 1974, all restrictions were off, and men and women were both hired and promoted by the same rules.

Sgt. Carl W. Setser joined the force on September 15, 1952, and was killed on August 13, 1971. On that day, Setser and specialist Robert Kramer headed out to serve a search warrant for property stolen in a robbery. While collecting the evidence at 222 East Central Parkway, they pushed a disabled car and transported the heavy boxes of seized property. Setser suffered a massive heart attack and died.

Howard Smith joined the Cincinnati police force on November 1, 1940, and was killed on September 13, 1972. On December 30, 1971, Smith was working a protection detail at the Fifth Third Bank. During a robbery attempt by Raymond Sams and Isaac Beasley, 19 and 17 years old, respectively, Smith was shot in the head. He lay in General Hospital for eight and a half months before passing away.

The police force has always drawn in family participation. In these photographs stand, from left to right, officer Ed Scholl in 1918, officer Art Scholl Sr. in 1955, and officer Art Scholl Jr. in 1972. Ed, a charter member of the FOP, Queen City Lodge No. 69, was a Cincinnati officer; Art Sr. and Art Jr. were both Elmwood police officers. Art Jr. worked as an officer from March 28, 1928, to August 21, 1961.

Patrolmen William Brown (left) and Ray Scarloto (right) chat with area kids in March 1973. Brown was a police recruit in 1965 and worked until retirement in 1991. Upon retiring, his district captain commented, "Another good officer leaving us." Scarloto joined the police department as a recruit in 1969 and worked in District 1 for 10 years. He transferred to District 3 and retired from that district in 1995.

David L. Cole was appointed on July 20, 1969, and was killed in the line of duty on July 17, 1974. On that day around 12:40 a.m., Cole and Richard Newsom were dispatched to a report of a burglary in progress at the United Dairy Farmers (UDF) on 2372 Florence Avenue. Cole drove up Florence Avenue toward the store and stopped his vehicle near two males walking down the street. Roland Reaves, a 23 year old from Chicago, and Ricardo Woods, a 24 year old of Cincinnati, both shot Cole, who returned fire and fell to the ground injured. Reaves walked over to Cole, stood over him, and shot him as he lay on the ground. Cole died at 1:15 a.m. Reaves was arrested and sentenced to die by electrocution, but his death penalty was commuted to life imprisonment. Woods was arrested on July 19, 1974, in West Virginia. Woods was also sentenced to die by electrocution and also had his death penalty commuted to life. He was incarcerated until September 2, 1994, and released on parole. His whereabouts are unknown.

Three officers stand holding a plaque for fallen officer Cole. They are, from left to right, patrolman Walter Barlag, patrolman Tom Waller, and patrolman Stephen Hoerst. In 1975, Cole worked in District 7. As of 2007, this plaque now hangs in District 4 because of the consolidation of Districts 7 and 4. At this time, Waller commands the Background Investigation Unit, and Hoerst is retired.

Patrolman Jim Assum (left) and Lt. Col. William R. Bracke (center) stand with Mayor Theodore M. Berry in a photograph taken in July 1974. After recruit school in 1952, Bracke was assigned to District 4. He attended multiple police classes at the FBI Academy. He retired from the Investigations Bureau in 1986. Assum was a cadet in 1967 and retired in 1995. His father, Paul Assum, was also a policeman.

Charles F. Handorf was appointed September 15, 1952, and died December 8, 1974. On that day around 1:45 a.m., Handorf and other officers surrounded a house on Home City Avenue where 38-year-old Herbert Merz had barricaded himself in. Merz shot and killed Handorf; the other officers returned fire, killing Merz. Handorf was transported to General Hospital by officers Phemann and Rinear, where Handorf was pronounced dead. He left a wife.

William J. Loftin was appointed September 25, 1966, and died on August 26, 1975. On that day at 10:45 p.m. Loftin found Cleophus Collins, the 53-year-old suspect of discharging a firearm at a bar. Collins shot Loftin with a handgun and killed him. Officers Robb and Payton arrested Collins, who was tried and sentenced to die in the electric chair. The sentence later was commuted to life.

Robert A. Lally was appointed on June 18, 1956, and killed on December 8, 1975. That day at 12:55 a.m., Lally was checking the rear business entrance at 5552 Colerain Avenue just as 30-year-old Richard Strunk came out the door. Thinking Lally was a burglar, he shot him. Strunk was arrested and charged with involuntary manslaughter. In May 1976, Strunk was sentenced to prison and paroled on April 19, 1977.

A sculptor finishes up his sculpture in his own studio. The statue originally stood outside District 1, but currently resides outside of the Greater Cincinnati Police Historical Society Museum, located at 959 West Eighth Street. A plaque on the bottom of the sculpture reads, "Erected through the effort of the Queen City Ladies Auxilary #9 to the FOP, 1975."

Capt. William "Bull" Neal was known for his booming voice and humorous sayings. Bull joined the air force in 1941 and stayed there until 1945. He then joined the CPD on December 1, 1945, and quickly rose through the ranks, including an assignment on the burglary and intelligence squad in the Crime Bureau. He also worked at District 5 as a relief commander until his promotion to captain in September 1972. As captain, he was the night chief until January 1973, when he was transferred to commanding officer. He retired in June 1976 at that position. He was also a successful wrestler—on January 1, 1977, he was appointed to the Cincinnati Boxing and Wrestling Commission by then–city manager William V. Donaldson. He also worked as secretary of that organization for many years, ensuring wrestling fights around town went off without a hitch.

Four

Modern-Day Police Department 1977–2007

Here police chief Myron Jack Leistler gives an interview. Leistler served as chief from 1976 to 1985—he succeeded Carl Goodin, who stepped down. Leistler, known to have impeccable character, was chosen to replace Goodin to restore high moral standards to the police department. Nicknamed "Gingerale Jack" because he did not drink, Leistler took a strict military approach to reforming the department and was applauded for his efforts.

Sgt. James Brunck presents an award to police specialist Diane Arnold (left) and Cheryl Grant (right). Arnold joined the force on September 15, 1968, and became one of the first of four women assigned to the formerly all-male homicide squad in 1975. It is interesting to note that when Arnold and her female cohorts joined the squad, one investigator requested a transfer so he did not have to work with females. But Arnold (nicknamed Peaches) later made headlines in 1978 for her good investigative work with the senior member of the squad at that time, Thomas Gardner (nicknamed Pickles). Grant grew up in the Lincoln Park area and joined the force August 1968. Grant was the third African American female to join the force, and she worked alongside Novella Noble, one of the first African American women to accomplish this task along with Lillian Grigsby (both joined in 1947). Grant joined 21 years later, after Noble and Grigsby, and resigned in 1970.

In this photograph, taken around 1973, from left to right are (first row) Kathleen Droder, Lillian Grigsby, Novella Noble, Helen Seiler, and Ruth Weller; (second row) Connie Breitbeil, Donna Ritter-Kim, Mary Zieverink-Hosinski, Pat Whalen-Herron, Louise Shelley, Grace Joan Hoffman-Crawford, Terry Armstrong, Diane Arnold, Marvelle Vonderhaar, and Phyllis Caskey. Weller was among the first females on the force; Wanda Basham, Elizabeth Pack, and Lucy Rankin were also hired in 1945.

During Crime Prevention Week in 1976 to honor officer Robert Apple, a policeman in District 6, Joe Staft addresses listeners at the Exchange Club Luncheon. Staft quickly rose through the police ranks. He took, and excelled at, all the tests for higher ranks after the minimum required number of years to take those tests. He retired as an assistant chief.

During the 1970s, a band called Night Beat was started, featuring musicians who were also policemen. Members included these five officers pictured here, from left to right, Bob Morgan, William Couch, Joe Staft, Bob Smith, and Michael Hill, who also played backup for James Brown. Other officers in the group included John Thomas, Alan Matthews, and Tony Krueger.

Melvin Thurman, one of the first African American police officer motorcyclists, entered the service in January 1956 and retired January 1986. While in uniform, he worked as a patrol officer, automobile accident investigator, motorcycle officer, recruiter, and old clothes (another name for undercover work). He was nicknamed the "three-wheeled man" because he drove a three-wheel motorcycle, nicknamed the "Servi-Car."

In speaking with Melvin Thurman, he said that he loved being on the three-wheel motorcycle, two of which are shown leading this parade. Police officers could ride these sturdy bikes year-round, where as the men on the two-wheel motorcycles had to hang them up during the winter. His time on the force inspired a lifelong love for the open road for Thurman.

Two motorcyclists—officer Jerry Thomas can be seen riding his motorcycle in the front—lead the way in a police memorial parade. Nick Guerrera also marches next to the FOP flag. This photograph was taken on Central Parkway near Lincoln Park Drive (now Ezzard Charles Drive).

Charles D. Burdsall was appointed on December 29, 1972, and died in the line of duty on July 15, 1978. On that day at 12:10 a.m., Burdsall stopped a vehicle suspected in an armed robbery minutes before at the King Kwik convenience store at McMicken and Dixmyth Avenues. As he approached the car, he was shot by either Wayne Reed or Russell Bell, both inside the car. A police cadet riding with Burdsall ran from the passenger side of the police cruiser, pulled Burdsall's revolver, and shot at the suspects as the car pulled away. Several bullet holes in the car later helped identify Reed and Bell. Burdsall's brother, Donald Burdsall, retired as a lieutenant from the police department several years later. Both Reed and Bell were sentenced to die in the electric chair, but both sentences were commuted to life.

The Ohio Crime Prevention Association included, pictured from left to right, Sgt. Milton Dills, superintendent of the Ohio Highway Patrol Colonel Chiarimonte, Jose Higgins, and Tierney O'Rourke. Although based out of Columbus, the organization is an important educational tool for the CPD. Founded in 1977, this organization works with those in law enforcement, members of government agencies and corporations, and community members to develop policies, programs, and publications for statewide policing agencies. In 1979, they hosted their first training class, and the organization continues to offer training seminars and workshops on crime prevention and community relations. Also during this year, the CPD established their own panel to study safety equipment used by their officers. This focus group recommended equipping patrol vehicles with better spotlights and giving officers better flashlights, bullet-resistant vests, and .357 revolvers. Officers' sidearms were again improved the next year with the addition of the Smith and Wesson Model 65 .357 revolvers with four-inch barrels loaded with .38 Special +P+ cartridges.

Robert T. Seiffert was appointed February 28, 1971, and was killed on March 6, 1979. Around 1:00 a.m., Seiffert stopped a vehicle driven by Gregory Daniels, a 28 year old wanted for aggravated robbery from December 1978. Seiffert was hit by Daniels's second shot, which hit him in the head as he dove for cover behind the car. Officer Art Evans was the first officer on the scene. Seiffert, still alive, was taken to Bethesda Oak Hospital (one block from the shooting). He died and was pronounced by Dr. Greiner at 3:09 a.m. He was transported to the morgue by officer Tom VonLeuhrte. Dennis Bennington was taken to Bethesda Oak Hospital, but his injuries were irreparable. He died and was pronounced by Dr. Gonzalez, at 2:27 a.m. He was transported to the morgue by officer Mike Broering. Sharon Johnson, a passenger in Daniels's car, was slightly wounded in the incident.

Bennington was appointed on October 29, 1972, and killed in the line of duty on March 6, 1979, with officer Seiffert. Bennington, covering Seiffert, approached the driver's door, while Seiffert approached from the rear. Daniels shot Bennington in the chest, knocking him down. Bennington got up, drew his revolver, and fired at Daniels as he pulled away, striking Daniels in the head and killing him instantly.

Melvin Henze was appointed on February 28, 1971, and killed on May 5, 1979. At 1:30 p.m., Henze was driving after Percy Wilson, a 28 year old wanted for felonious assault, running on foot. Wilson jumped out from behind a building and shot Henze five times in the upper body through his open car window. Officers Nick Misch and Wes Sullivan arrested Wilson, who was sentenced to 22 years to life.

James Gary Weber, who went by his middle name, was appointed September 8, 1974, and was killed in the line of duty on September 8, 1982. On that day at 11:35 p.m., at 2787 River Road, officers Weber and Charles Klug were investigating a suspicious automobile. Stephen James, a 35-year-old highly intoxicated male, was driving his Chevrolet Corvette at high speeds inbound on River Road. He struck the parked car that the officers were investigating and caught them between his car and the parked car. The Corvette careened off the parked car, carrying Weber with it, and slammed into a utility pole. Weber was killed instantly, and Klug suffered massive injuries, including two nearly detached legs. James was arrested by officer Roger Smallwood of the Traffic Section. Klug retired and continues to require operations. He later came back to work as a police technician and retired again during 2005. James was charged with aggravated vehicular homicide, convicted, and sentenced to one and a half years in prison.

Citizens visit the police auction in the city hall courtyard for great deals on unclaimed goods. This picture was probably taken in the 1950s. Another auction opportunity open to the public is a biweekly automobile auction held on the first and third Saturday of each month at 3425 Spring Grove Avenue. In the 1960s and 1970s, Sgt. Joe Kline, nicknamed "Clear 'em out Joe," presided over the police impound lot, which is in charge of selling the cars. At that time, the impound lot was located on Gest Street. Kline noted some special items they confiscated in his day: a 1929 Lincoln, a 10-ton dump truck, customized vans aplenty, and numerous luxury cars. He also noted that an average of 110 vehicles were brought in each week.

Officer Gene Simpkins was the official police property auctioneer from 1971 to 1985. A professional auctioneer, Simpkins worked at the auction and as a school resource officer at Western Hills High School. During this time, the property auctions were held twice a year in the parking lot in the center of city hall. As of 2007, property auctions are held online at PropertyBureau.com.

Fr. Bruno Kremp is a Cincinnati Franciscan priest. Since 1967, he has served as a volunteer chaplain for the Hamilton County Sheriff's Office, and in 1980, he helped found a team of chaplains for the Hamilton County Police Association. This team serves not only the CPD but also other agencies throughout the county. The group helps officers when the job seems overwhelming as well as police families under stress.

Clifford W. George was appointed October 24, 1971, and died in the line of duty on April 16, 1987. On that day at 1:06 a.m., George responded to a domestic complaint about 33-year-old Melvin Moreland. A struggle ensued, and Moreland, who had cocaine in his system, took George's weapon from his holster and shot him. George fell to his knees mortally wounded. Moreland shot at witnesses twice, then picked up George by the collar of his shirt and shot him again in the back of the neck. Canine officer Gerald Norton and officer Steve Fromholt, with the canine Bandit, found Moreland, naked and still carrying George's sidearm. The officers ordered him to drop the firearm, but he raised the revolver toward the officers. Bandit lunged at Moreland, and all three humans fired revolvers. Both Bandit and Moreland were killed. George left wife Barbara, son Jeff, and daughters Jennifer and Paige. Jennifer became a police officer in July 1998. After George's death, officers were issued nine millimeter semiautomatic pistols and security holsters. No Cincinnati officer has been killed with his own sidearm since.

Here stand members of the mountain bike patrol at the Police Memorial at Ezzard Charles Drive. They are, from left to right, Jamel Smith, Joy Ludgatis, Steve Saunders, Tomas DeFosse, and Mark Fowler. This patrol was a dream of Andy Hayden's. In 1992, Hayden was working towards his masters in criminal justice at the University of Cincinnati. Since he loved riding mountain bikes, for his thesis he researched and wrote a mountain bike patrol pilot program for the CPD. He presented his work to then–police chief Michael Snowden, who agreed to initiate the program in 1993 in District 4. The bike patrol was so successful within those first six months that Snowden agreed to make this a full-time department. As of 2007, there are more than 50 mountain bike officers, which grew from an original patrol of eight officers and four mountain bikes.

Seen here are more mountain bike patrol officers, including, from left to right, Steve Saunders, Mark Fowler, David Simpson, Thomas DeFosse, Jennifer Ventre, and Joy Judgatis. Hayden left the Cincinnati police in May 1995 for a position in the FBI, and Sgt. Dave Simpson took over training responsibilities.

Dan Mitchell sits in front of the motorcycle police memorial in 1996. The image of the motorcyclist in this memorial was styled after motorcycle patrolman Robert Leigh, who died on Reading Road. Leigh was riding to city hall for an off-duty roll call when Dale Ettor pulled out from a driveway and hit Leigh with his car. Leigh, a six-year-veteran motorcycle officer, was a bass drummer in the department's drum corps.

Police officers stand with Bob Dole at Lunken Airport during his visit to Cincinnati during the 1996 U.S. presidential election. Richard Gross, who was then working protection detail in the Criminal Investigation Unit, stands on the far left of the picture, next to other officers, Ken Johnson, Scott Fritz, and Mike Temple, from the Burglary, Fraud, and Criminalistics Unit. Gross joined the force in 1974 and worked at District 7 for many years. In the background is Tom Steidel, a retired fire chief.

Just before midnight, on December 5, 1997, specialist Ron Jeter (pictured here) and officer Daniel Pope searched for and found Alonzo Davenport, a 19-year-old male wanted for felony domestic violence. Jeter and Pope arrested Davenport, who had concealed a revolver in the small of his back. Davenport pulled the revolver and shot each officer once in the head, killing both instantly.

Specialist Jeter and his partner, officer Pope (pictured here), found Davenport at 23 West Hollister in Clifton Heights, a few blocks north of where the last slain Cincinnati officer, Cliff George, was killed 10 years earlier. After shooting both officers, Davenport ran from the scene. When he saw other officers at Vine and McMillan Streets, he killed himself with a gunshot to the head.

Police officers and citizens stand at attention for the funeral procession for officer Pope. Pope left his father, Robert, a retired police officer; mother; and wife, Linda, a Cincinnati firefighter. Jeter, a former U.S. Marine, often read Shakespeare and was known for his easygoing personality. He left a mother, fiancée, and children. His funeral procession headed up I-71 to his hometown of Columbus.

Police officer Kevin Crayon was killed in the line of duty on September 1, 2000. On that day, Crayon saw a young male (later identified as a 12 year old) getting in to drive a car in the UDF parking lot at Colerain and Kirby Avenues. Kevin ordered him to stop, but the youth backed the car toward some children and their mother in the parking lot. Kevin ran to, and reached into the car to stop it. He was successful, but then the youth drove forward onto Colerain Avenue with the officer in tow. Crayon was dragged some 800 feet, then shot the youth and was released from the car. Crayon was killed instantly as he rolled under a car stopped in traffic. The youth struck another car and continued to his home, where his family called emergency medical services. The youth died of his wound a few hours later. Crayon, a U.S. Army veteran, left his mother, Barbara Crayon Allbright, three brothers, a sister, and three children, Kevin II, Christopher, and Brittany.

In 2001, riots again gripped the city. This time, they were sparked by the fatal shooting of a 19-year-old African American male, Timothy Thomas, at Republic Street (shown here) near Thirteenth Street. Steven Roach, a Caucasian police officer, shot Thomas at 2:20 a.m. on April 7, during an on-foot pursuit by several officers. Again citing racial tension as the main cause of their anger, citizens took action. On April 9, 2001, approximately 175 residents protested during a city council committee meeting, asking for the details of Thomas's death. A few days later, Charlie Luken—then mayor of Cincinnati—issued a curfew. The rioting died down by April 13 of that year. It is estimated an ensuing boycott of downtown businesses caused a loss of more than $10 million in convention and entertainment revenue. After this incident, the city agreed to the following initiatives: first, form a community focus group (later named Community-Police Oriented Policing); second, revise their use-of-force policies; and third, create a citizen-complaint panel independent of the police.

Taken at the August 2004 National Underground Railroad Freedom Center, retired police lieutenant Joe Hall poses with Muhammed Ali. Assigned as part of Ali's protection detail, Hall says Ali was an amateur magician who performed magic tricks for the group and tried to encourage Hall to spar with him. Hall joined the force in 1967 and worked at Districts 1 and 4, in research and planning, the Juvenile Bureau, and intelligence. Hall says his job in intelligence was to plan for visits from notables and to work in conjunction with the secret service or other agencies to make sure the people they protected remained safe. The typical process is to pair up one Cincinnati officer with one secret service officer in the same car. Since arrest powers and communication lines were different, having one of each type of officer made it possible to meet any emergency. Hall himself spent 19 years with that department, and helped protect Ronald Reagan, Richard Nixon, Bill Clinton, George H. W. Bush, and George W. Bush.

Standing here are, from left to right, unidentified, O'dell Owens (the Hamilton County coroner of Cincinnati), and Cincinnati mayor Mark Mallory at the Greater Cincinnati Police Historical Society Museum's grand opening in June 2006. Located at 959 West Eighth Street, Suite 201, this museum holds police memorabilia dating back to the 1800s for all law enforcement in the tristate area, including the Cincinnati police, Hamilton County police, and the Ohio State Highway Patrol. The museum boasts displays of handguns and other weapons police have used throughout the years. And, as a regional museum, they also have on hand more than 40 uniforms of suburban police departments, including Delhi, Carthage, College Hill, Madisonville, Mount Airy, Sayler Park, Madeira, Montgomery, and Sharonville, all of which were incorporated into Cincinnati between 1910 and 1911. The museum is also a great place for police force veterans and their families to stop by and chat with other retired members or museum volunteers. They also offer tours.

During the Greater Cincinnati Police Historical Society Museum grand opening in June 2006, special guests include, from left to right, Kenton County sheriff Charles Korzenborn; Randy Lofsping, the owner of Roy Tailors Uniform Company, a Cincinnati-based business that specializes in making police uniforms; and Cincinnati police chief Tom Streicher Jr. All were on hand to celebrate the big day including Hamilton County sheriff Simon L. Leis Jr.

In August 2006, early female officers reunited to talk about their experiences and help record them for future generations. All were appointed between 1945 and 1982, and many served through 2002. They reminisced about many things, including the official "purse" they had to carry while on duty. This 15-pound purse held their chemical spray, police pistol, and radio. It was the first of its kind in the country.

Lillian Grigsby, shown here in August 2006, followed in her father's footsteps when she signed up for the academy. Her father, Robert A. Wilson, served on the police department from 1925 to 1947, then died from an illness. Grigsby received his same badge number, No. 641, when she graduated from recruit class later that year.

Simon L. Leis Jr. the 2007 Hamilton County sheriff, served with the U.S. Marine Corps until 1960 and, in 1987, was appointed to serve an unexpired term as sheriff. In 1988, 1992, 1996, 2000, and 2004, he was reelected to four-year terms as sheriff. As sheriff, he was in charge of much of the equipment used by local agencies, including a helicopter.

On Saturday, February 24, 2007, the Greater Cincinnati Police Historical Society Museum hosted an event for Black History Month celebrating past African American officers and their achievements. From left to right sit Handy Matthews, Melvin Thurman, Clayton David (a Hamilton County officer), Cecil Thomas, and Lillian Grigsby. All of these distinguished officers were recognized for their career achievements and contributions.

At this ceremony, councilman Cecil Thomas (right) was awarded the first Frank A. B. Hall award. Presenting the award is Richard Gross, a Greater Cincinnati Police Historical Society member. Thomas joined Cincinnati's city council (in 2005) after working 27 years as a Cincinnati officer. He was given the award because his career path resembles that of Hall, an African American police officer in the late 19th century who later joined Cincinnati's city council.

Col. Thomas H. Streicher Jr., the 2007 police chief, joined the Cincinnati police force as a cadet in 1971. In 1975, he graduated from the police academy and became a patrolman. He continued rising through the ranks and was promoted to police specialist in 1981, sergeant in 1985, lieutenant in 1988, and district captain in 1993. He became the lieutenant colonel (assistant police chief) in January 1998, and was promoted in March 1999 to police chief. He also serves on many local boards and commissions, including the Bridges for a Just Community; the Ohio Law Enforcement Foundation; the Boy Scouts of America Daniel Beard Council; Downtown Cincinnati, Incorporated; and the Hamilton County Criminal Justice Commission. Throughout his career, he worked as an undercover drug investigator, special operations unit commander, and SWAT commander.